CIMA EXAMINATION KIT

Foundation Level

Paper 3a

Economics for Business

GW00601960

ISBN 1 84390 292 3

British Library Cataloguing-in-Publication data

A catalogue record for this book is available from the British Library.

We are grateful to the Chartered Institute of Management Accountants for permission to reproduce past assessment material. The solutions have been prepared by The Financial Training Company.

Published by

The Financial Training Company
4 The Griffin Centre
Staines Road
Feltham
Middlesex TW14 0HS

All rights reserved. No part of this publication may be reproduced, stored in a retrieval system, or transmitted, in any form or by any means, electronic, mechanical, photocopying, recording or otherwise, without the prior written permission of The Financial Training Company.

© The Financial Training Company 2004

Contents

	Question	*Answer*

Questions and Answers

Introduction

This examination kit and attached CD is designed to prepare you for the new style computer based assessment for Paper 3a Economics for Business.

Notes from CIMA

We reproduce below notes from CIMA regarding these new style assessments.

What types of questions are used?

Objective questions are used. The most common type is 'multiple choice', where students have to choose the correct answer from a list of possible answers.

There are a variety of other objective question types that can be used within the system. These include true/false questions, matching pairs of text and graphic, sequencing and ranking, labelling diagrams, and single and multiple numeric entry.

Students will answer the questions by either pointing and clicking the mouse, moving objects around the screen, typing numbers, or a combination of these responses. An **online demo** is also available.

The questions for each assessment are randomly selected from a large question bank; the question bank is regularly reviewed. There are also randomisation processes within individual questions. The CBA system can ensure that a wide range of the syllabus is assessed, as a pre-determined number of questions from each syllabus area (dependent upon the syllabus study weighting for that particular area) are selected in each assessment.

The time allowed for each CBA is outlined below:

♦   Financial Accounting Fundamentals – 90 minutes (comprising 40 questions with one or more parts).

♦   Management Accounting Fundamentals – 90 minutes (comprising 40 questions with one or more parts).

♦   Economics for Business – 60 minutes (comprising 40 questions with one or more parts).

♦   Business Law – 60 minutes (comprising 40 questions with one or more parts).

♦   Business Mathematics – 90 minutes (comprising 35 questions with one or more parts).

Style of questions in this kit

We have included styles of questions which you will not meet in the assessment itself, because this kit serves two functions:

(a)   Questions which will assist and reinforce the learning process itself.

(b)   Questions which will prepare you for the precise type of question you will meet in the examination.

The kit is therefore produced in three parts:

(a)   Part 1 – objective test questions. These may be longer than some of the questions you will get in the examination but will include the main assessment techniques (eg true/false, filling answers in a box, etc). The fact that they are longer than the examination questions will reinforce your knowledge, and help you understand how the concepts fit together.

(b)   Part 2 – multiple choice questions. Whilst these are not the only form of objective test questions that the examiner will set, CIMA have indicated that multiple choice questions will be 'the most common type' of objective test question used.

These multiple choice questions are therefore the most likely questions you will meet in the examination.

(c)   Part 3 – mock examination CD. This CD replicates precisely the style of computer based assessment which you will meet in your CIMA examination. The screens and the operations you can perform on the screens are exactly the same as those in the CIMA examination. Obviously, the questions are different.

We suggest that you work through this CD when you have completed all the other elements of this kit.

Multiple choice questions

The multiple choice questions will comprise a question with four possible answers. For example,

1 What is the world's tallest mountain?

    A Ben Nevis

    B K2

    C Mount Everest

    D Mount Snowdon

You have to select the correct answer (which in the above example is of course **C**).

In the examination, however, the incorrect answers, called distractors, may be quite plausible and are sometimes designed if not exactly to mislead you, they may nevertheless be the result of fairly common mistakes.

The following is a suggested technique for answering these questions, but as you practise for the examination you have to work out a method which suits you.

Step 1

Read all the questions, but not necessarily the answers. Select the ones which you think are the most straightforward and do them first.

Step 2

For more awkward questions, some people prefer to work the question without reference to the answers which increases your confidence if your answer then matches one of the options. However some people prefer to view the question with the four answers as this may assist them in formulating their answer.

This is a matter of personal preference and you should perhaps practise each to see which you find most effective.

Step 3

If your answer does not match one of the options you must:

(a) Re-read the question carefully to make sure you have not missed some important point.

(b) Re-work your solution eliminating any mistakes.

(c) Beware the plausible distractors but do not become paranoid. The examiner is not trying to trip you up and the answer should be a straightforward calculation from the question.

Step 4

Time allocation. As with all questions you must not overrun your time. The questions are technically worth only two marks each which is about three to four minutes per question. It is very easy to get bogged down. If you cannot get one of the right answers then move on to the next question.

Step 5

When you have finished all the questions go back to the ones you have not answered.

Keep an eye on the clock – don't overrun the time allocation.

If you really cannot do it, **have a guess**. You are not penalised for wrong answers. **Never leave any questions unanswered.**

Syllabus

Syllabus overview

This syllabus is designed to enable students to acquire a knowledge and understanding of the fundamental economic concepts necessary for the work of the Chartered Management Accountant.

Aims

This syllabus aims to test the student's ability to:

♦ identify how a market economy functions and the role of government within it;

♦ explain the economic environment within which businesses operate;

♦ identify the economic factors which influence the behaviour and performance of firms and industries;

♦ prepare the economic analysis that informs and guides the advice given to business decision-makers.

Assessment

There will be a 60 minute computer based assessment comprising 40 questions with one or more parts.

Learning outcomes and syllabus content

3a(i) The Economy and the growth of Economic Welfare – 10%

Learning outcomes

On completion of their studies students should be able to:

♦ Explain the principal issues related to economic welfare and its growth.

♦ Explain the main trends in the rate and structure of economic growth in recent years.

♦ Explain the central economic problem and the concepts of scarcity and opportunity cost.

♦ Explain the main factors determining the rate of economic growth.

♦ Explain the main elements of government policy towards economic growth.

Syllabus content

♦ The concept of economic welfare.

♦ Economic growth: trends in economic growth; factors in economic growth.

♦ Economic welfare and sustainable growth.

♦ Issues in economic growth and growth policy.

3a(ii) The market system and the competitive process – 40%

Learning outcomes

On completion of their studies students should be able to:

♦ Explain the functioning of a market economy.

♦ Explain how the price system works by applying appropriate economic concepts and principles.

♦ Explain and illustrate how product and factor markets operate.

♦ Apply basic economic analysis to explain economic and business issues.

♦ Explain the behaviour of business costs in both the short and long run.

♦ Explain the economic factors which affect the structure, behaviour and performance of individual businesses and industries.

♦ Analyse the process of competition in different market structures.

♦ Identify the public issues that are raised by business activity.

♦ Explain how governments might respond to the effects of business on the environment.

Syllabus content

♦ The business environment and the structure of economic activity.

♦ Business firms: legal, economic and organisational features; entrepreneurship and profit.

♦ Business functions: production and costs, finance and marketing.

♦ The market process: supply and demand and their determinants.

♦ The price mechanism: the demand and supply model and its applications.

♦ Forms of market structure: competition and economic welfare; competition policy; regulation and deregulation; the public sector and privatisation.

♦ Business and the environment; externalities and public policy.

3a(iii) The macroeconomic framework – 30%

Learning outcomes

On completion of their studies students should be able to:

♦ Identify the appropriate macroeconomic concepts to explain the measurement and determination of national income

♦ Explain macroeconomic phenomena by demonstrating a simple circular flow of income model.

♦ Identify the main indicators of macroeconomic performance and demonstrate their significance.

♦ Identify the main elements of the monetary and financial system.

♦ Explain the importance of the monetary environment to the business sector.

♦ Explain the economic role of government through fiscal and monetary policy and demonstrate the impact of such policies on the business sector.

♦ Explain the nature of the trade cycle, its causes and consequences.

♦ Explain the debates concerning the nature of the macro-economy and appropriate government policy.

Syllabus content

♦ National income: its measurement and determination; the circular flow of income and a simple aggregate demand and supply model; unemployment and the price level.

♦ The monetary environment: inflation and the money supply; the banking and financial system; interest rates and monetary policy.

♦ The fiscal environment: taxation and public spending; the budget and government borrowing; demand management and supply side policy.

♦ Macroeconomic stability; economic fluctuations and their causes; macroeconomic forecasting and stabilisation policy.

3a(iv) The open economy – 20%

Learning outcomes

On completion of their studies students should be able to:

♦ Explain patterns of international trade and the sources of international specialisation.

♦ Identify the international movement of factors of production and the role of transnational companies in this process.

♦ Identify and explain the concept and consequences of globalisation for businesses and national economies.

♦ Explain the concept of the balance of payments and its determinants.

♦ Distinguish between different exchange rate regimes and explain their implications for the business sector.

♦ Identify the main elements of national policy with respect to external economic relations, especially in the context of regional trading blocs.

Syllabus content

♦ Patterns of international trade and trade policy; regional trading blocs; the globalisation of production.

♦ International factor movements; international capital markets; international investment flows; the movement of labour and technology; the nature and role of transnational companies.

♦ The balance of payments; structure and determinants of the balance of payments; foreign exchange markets and exchange rate regimes; European monetary union.

Meaning of CIMA's examination requirements

CIMA use precise words in the requirements of their questions. In the schedule below we reproduce the precise meanings of these words from the CIMA syllabus. You must learn these definitions and make sure that in the exam you do precisely what CIMA requires you to do.

Learning objective	Verbs used	Definition
1 Knowledge What you are expected to know	List	Make a list of
	State	Express, fully or clearly, the details of/facts of
	Define	Give the exact meaning of
2 Comprehension What you are expected to understand	Describe	Communicate the key features of
	Distinguish	Highlight the differences between
	Explain	Make clear or intelligible/state the meaning of
	Identify	Recognise, establish or select after consideration
	Illustrate	Use an example to describe or explain something
3 Application Can you apply your knowledge?	Apply	To put to practical use
	Calculate/compute	To ascertain or reckon mathematically
	Demonstrate	To prove with certainty or to exhibit by practical means
	Prepare	To make or get ready for use
	Reconcile	To make or prove consistent/compatible
	Solve	Find an answer to
	Tabulate	Arrange in a table
4 Analysis Can you analyse the detail of what you have learned?	Analyse	Examine in detail the structure of
	Categorise	Place into a defined class or division
	Compare and contrast	Show the similarities and/or differences between
	Construct	To build up or compile
	Discuss	To examine in detail by argument
	Interpret	To translate into intelligible or familiar terms
	Produce	To create or bring into existence
5 Evaluation Can you use your learning to evaluate, make decisions or recommendations?	Advise	To counsel, inform or notify
	Evaluate	To appraise or assess the value of
	Recommend	To advise on a course of action

Objective Test Questions

Question 1

The following diagram shows production possibility frontiers (PPF) for an economy:

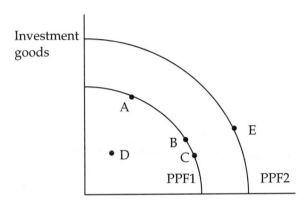

Required

(a)   Using your knowledge of economic theory and the diagram above, complete the following statements:

   (i)   Opportunity cost is...

   (Your answer must not exceed 20 words)

(2 marks)

   (ii)   Opportunity cost can be demonstrated from production possibility frontier 1 (PPF1) by a move ....

   (Your answer must not exceed 15 words)

(2 marks)

(Total for part (a) : 4 marks)

(b)   Fill in the gaps in the following sentence (one word for each gap):

The move from point A to point B shows the amount of investment goods that have to be _____ to acquire more _____ goods.

(1 mark for each word)

(Total for part (b) : 2 marks)

(c)   Describe the features of the diagram that illustrate;

(i)   the existence of unemployment in the economy;

(Your answer must not exceed 20 words)

(2 marks)

(ii)   the process of economic growth;

(Your answer must not exceed 15 words)

(2 marks)

(Total for part (c) : 4 marks)

(d)   State two sources of economic growth.

(Each answer must not exceed 8 words)

(i)   _____   **(1 mark)**

(ii)   _____   **(1 mark)**

(Total for part (d) : 2 marks)

(e)   (i)   Explain what the term 'productivity' means.

(Your answer must not exceed 10 words)

(1 mark)

(ii)   Give three examples of how productivity can be increased.

(Each answer must not exceed 10 words)

(1)   **(1 mark)**

(2)   **(1 mark)**

(3)   **(1 mark)**

(Total for part (e) : 4 marks)

(Question total : 16 marks)

Question 2

The following data refer to the cost and revenue schedules of a business.

Quantity sold	Price £	Total cost £
0	-	12
1	16	20
2	14	25
3	12	30
4	10	34
5	8	45
6	6	66
7	4	110

Required

(a)   Using your knowledge of economic theory and the information above, complete the following table.

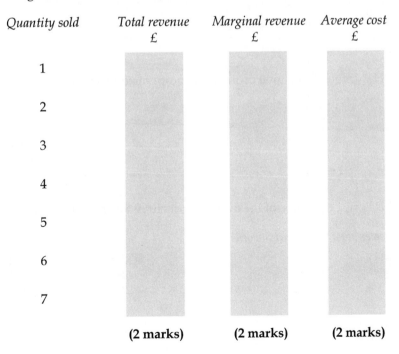

Quantity sold	Total revenue £	Marginal revenue £	Average cost £
1			
2			
3			
4			
5			
6			
7			

(2 marks)   **(2 marks)**   **(2 marks)**

(Total for part (a) : 6 marks)

(b)   (i)   Complete the following statement:

Price elasticity of demand is....

(Your answer must not exceed 15 words)

(1 mark)

(ii)   Calculate the price elasticity of demand for a price rise from £10 to £12.

(2 marks)

(Total for part (b) : 3 marks)

(c)   (i)   Fill in the gaps in the following sentence (two words to each gap).

Profits are maximised at the output level where   equals   .

(1 mark for each pair of words)

(2 marks)

(ii)   Using the information given in the data above, what is the profit maximising level of sales?

(1 mark)

(iii)   How much is the total profit at the profit maximising level of sales?

(1 mark)

(Total for part (c) : 4 marks)

(d)   (i)   Describe the shape of the average cost curve for this business.

(Your answer must not exceed 5 words)

(1 mark)

(ii)   Complete the following statement:

The law of diminishing returns to a fixed factor states that as successive units of a variable factor are added to a fixed factor…..

(Your answer must not exceed 15 words)

(2 marks)

(Total for part (d) : 3 marks)

(Question total : 16 marks)

Question 3

The following diagram shows the relationship between income and expenditure for an economy.

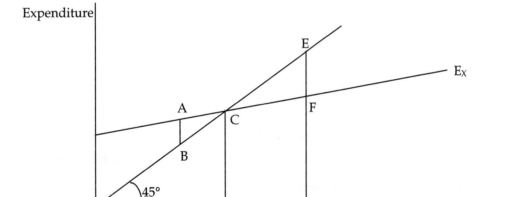

Required

(a)   Using your knowledge of economic theory and the diagram above, state what the following are:

(i)   the components of the expenditure curve;

(2 marks)

(ii)   the equilibrium level of national income;

(1 mark)

(iii)   the deflationary gap.

(1 mark)

(Total for part (a) : 4 marks)

(b)   State what would happen to the components of expenditure and the impact on the equilibrium level of national income in each of the following situations:

	Effect on the components Of expenditure	*Impact on the equilibrium level of national income*
(i) An increase in the marginal propensity to save	**(1 mark)**	**(1 mark)**
(ii) A move towards surplus on the current account of the balance of payments	**(1 mark)**	**(1 mark)**
(iii) A decrease in taxation	**(1 mark)**	**(1 mark)**
(iv) An increase in stockholding by businesses	**(1 mark)**	**(1 mark)**

(Total for part (b) : 8 marks)

(c)   State whether each of the following statements is true or false:

	Encircle your answer in each case	
If the government used interest rate policy to raise the equilibrium level of national income, they would reduce interest rates	*True or False*	**(1 mark)**
A reduction in interest rates will reduce consumption	*True or False*	**(1 mark)**
A reduction in interest rates will increase investment	*True or False*	**(1 mark)**

(Total for part (c) : 3 marks)

(d)   Explain one impact of a change in interest rates on the business sector.

(Your answer should not exceed 20 words)

(1 mark)

(Total for part (d) : 1 mark)

(Question total : 16 marks)

Question 4

The following data refer to a country's balance of payments accounts, measured in billions of pounds.

	Credits £bn	Debits £bn
Trade in goods	164	184
Trade in services	62	50
Investment income	114	98
Current transfers	15	21
Transfers of capital by government	1	0.7
Short term and long term investments	108	117

Required

(a)   Use your knowledge of economic theory and the data above to answer the following questions.

Which of the items shown above would be included in;

(i)   the calculation of the *current balance* of the balance of payments?

(2 marks)

(ii)   the *capital account* of the balance of payments?

(1 mark)

(iii)   the *financial account* of the balance of payments?

(1 mark)

(Total for part (a) : 4 marks)

(b)   Calculate the country's

(i)   balance of trade

(1 mark)

(ii)   current balance

(1 mark)

(iii)   adjusting item needed to balance the accounts

(1 mark)

(Total for part (b) : 3 marks)

(c)   Short term and long term investments can be *real* or *portfolio* investments. Explain what these terms mean.

(i)   Real investment...

(Your answer should not exceed 20 words)

(1 mark)

(ii)   Portfolio investment...

(Your answer should not exceed 20 words)

(1 mark)

(Total for part (c) : 2 marks)

(d)   State whether each of the following statements is true or false, if there is an appreciation (rise) in a country's exchange rate.

**Encircle your answer
in each case**

The foreign exchange price of exports will rise	*True or False*	**(1 mark)**
The domestic price of imports will fall	*True or False*	**(1 mark)**
If the demand for imports and exports is price elastic, the current account will move towards deficit	*True or False*	**(1 mark)**

(Total for part (d) = 3 marks)

(e)   Fill in the gaps in the following sentence (one word for each gap).

An appreciation in a country's currency will affect the costs of a business in that country. The costs of imported components or raw materials will ⬚. This will tend to ⬚ output prices. However, the demand for the business's output may ⬚ because imports become ⬚.

(1 mark for each word)

(Total for part (e) : 4 marks)

(Question total : 16 marks)

Question 5

The following diagram shows the cost structure of a firm for different sizes of factory (sizes 1-7) and their associated short run cost curves. These, taken together, make up the firm's long run average cost curve.

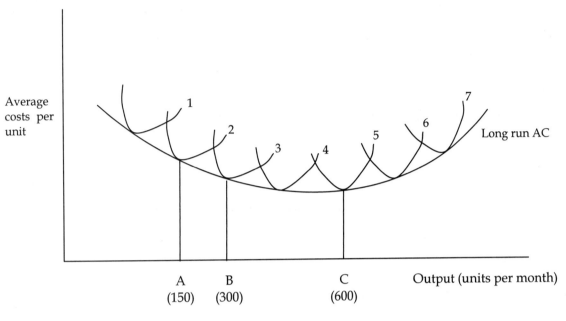

Required

(a)   Using your knowledge of economic theory and the diagram above, complete the following statements:

(i)   For a single firm, economies of scale are those factors which lead to ....

(Your answer must not exceed 15 words)

(2 marks)

(ii)   For a single firm, the short run average cost curve is U shaped because of the law of ....

(Your answer must not exceed 8 words)

(2 marks)

(Total for part (a) : 4 marks)

(b)   State three categories (types) of economies of scale for a single firm.

(Each answer must not exceed 5 words)

(i)   _____   **(1 mark)**

(ii)   _____   **(1 mark)**

(iii)   _____   **(1 mark)**

(Total for part (b) : 3 marks)

(c)   From the diagram:

(i)   define the cost characteristics of the range B – C;

(Your answer must not exceed 5 words)

_____   **(1 mark)**

(ii)   state the point where diseconomies of scale commence;

(Your answer must not exceed 5 words)

_____   **(1 mark)**

(iii)   state the most efficient scale of output to produce output level A;

(Your answer must not exceed 5 words)

_____   **(1 mark)**

(iv)   state what would be the most efficient way for this firm to produce 1200 units per month.

(Your answer must not exceed 15 words)

_____

(1 mark)

(Total for part (c) : 4 marks)

(d)   With respect to external economies of scale, fill in the gaps in the following sentence (one word for each gap):

External economies of scale lead to a reduction in the _____ of _____ when the size of the _____ increases.

(1 mark for each word)

(Total for part (d) : 3 marks)

(e)   State what would happen to the cost curves in the diagram if:

(i)   there were additional significant external economies of scale;

(Your answer must not exceed 15 words)

_____

(1 mark)

(ii)   technological change reduced the minimum efficient scale for this firm.

(Your answer must not exceed 15 words)

(1 mark)

(Total for part (e) : 2 marks)

(Question total : 16 marks)

Question 6

The following table shows some macroeconomic data for an imaginary economy. These are the percentage rates of inflation and unemployment and percentage increase in average earnings.

	Earnings (% increase)	Inflation (%)	Unemployment (%)
Year 1	6.1%	5.4%	3.9%
Year 2	5.8%	4.8%	4.5%
Year 3	4.2%	3.9%	6.1%
Year 4	2.2%	2.3%	6.8%
Year 5	2.1%	2.3%	6.9%
Year 6	2.5%	2.5%	6.8%
Year 7	3.0%	2.9%	6.2%
Year 8	3.4%	3.1%	5.9%
Year 9	4.3%	3.6%	5.4%
Year 10	4.8%	2.8%	5.0%
Year 11	4.7%	2.4%	4.5%
Year 12	4.5%	2.3%	4.3%

Required

(a)   Using your knowledge of economic theory and the table above

(i)   identify the years in which the standard of living fell;

(2 marks)

(ii)   state the percentage increase in real earnings in years 1 and 2.

Year 1   Year 2   **(1 mark each)**

(Total for part (a) : 4 marks)

(b)   (i)   From the table, state the apparent relationship between inflation and unemployment between years 1 and 8.

(Your answer must not exceed 15 words)

(2 marks)

(ii)   With respect to years 9 to 12, fill in the gaps in the following sentence (one word for each gap):

The relationship between inflation and unemployment in years 9 and 10 can be explained by a shift to the ▨▨▨▨▨ in the aggregate ▨▨▨▨▨ curve.

(1 mark for each word)

(Total for part (b) : 4 marks)

(c)   For each of the following possible sources of inflationary pressure, state whether it will lead to *demand pull inflation* or *cost push inflation*.

Encircle your answer in each case

(i)   an increase in the price of crude oil   *Demand pull or Cost push*   **(1 mark)**

(ii)   a reduction in the rate of income tax   *Demand pull or Cost push*   **(1 mark)**

(iii)   an increase in the rate of value added tax   *Demand pull or Cost push*   **(1 mark)**

(iv)   a rise in wage rates resulting from a
        general shortage of labour   *Demand pull or Cost push*   **(1 mark)**

(Total for part (c) : 4 marks)

(d)   State whether each of the following statements is *true* or *false*:

Encircle your answer in each case

(i)   inflation benefits businesses since prices
        always rise faster than costs   *True or False*   **(1 mark)**

(ii)   large debtors gain from the inflationary
        process   *True or False*   **(1 mark)**

(iii)   under flexible exchange rates inflation tends
        to damage the business sector's international
        competitiveness   *True or False*   **(1 mark)**

(iv)   to slow down inflation, the monetary authorities
        should raise interest rates   *True or False*   **(1 mark)**

(Total for part (d) : 4 marks)

(Question total : 16 marks)

Question 7

The following is based on an article in the *Financial Times* (22 March 1999)

Industry experts argue that, as a producer of little over half a million cars a year, however well made, attractive and profitable, BMW had no long-term future as an independent company. It is now, even after merging with Rover, the smallest of the world's significant car manufacturers. Over time, larger companies with economies of scale, will be able to surpass BMW quality and squeeze its profits. BMW's gamble on merging with Rover was to become big enough to survive.

BMW: a luxury minnow among whales

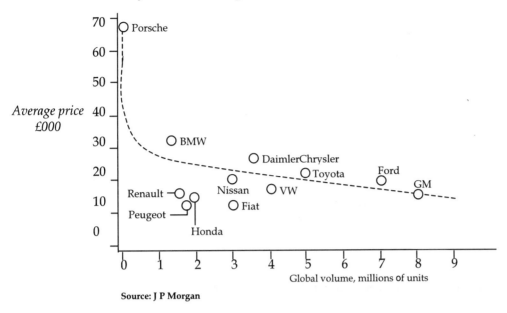

Source: J P Morgan

Required

(a)   Using both your knowledge of economic theory and the diagram and information above, complete the following statements:

(i)   minimum efficient scale is the ....

(Your answer must not exceed 15 words)

(2 marks)

(ii)   x-efficiency involves the use of a firm's factors of production .....

(Your answer must not exceed 15 words)

(2 marks)

(Total for part (a) : 4 marks)

(b)   (i)   What does the dotted line in the diagram reflect?

(Your answer must not exceed 10 words)

(1 mark)

(ii)   Assuming that prices and costs in the car industry are similar, at what output level in the diagram is the minimum efficient scale for the car industry reached?

(1 mark)

(iii)   Name one firm that appears to:

        (a)   have a high degree of x-efficiency   **(1 mark)**

        (b)   have a low degree of x-efficiency   **(1 mark)**

(iv)   With respect to x-efficiency, fill in the gaps in the following sentence (one word for each gap).

The most x-efficient firms are the ones in the diagram which are   the dotted line. This is because they have   than average, average   for the industry.

(1 mark for each word)

(Total for part (b) : 7 marks)

(c)   If BMW was to merge with Rover, it might gain from economies of scale.

    (i)   State three types/categories of economies of scale:

        (a)   **(1 mark)**

        (b)   **(1 mark)**

        (c)   **(1 mark)**

(ii)   Give two examples of economies of scale:

(Your answer must not exceed 5 words)

        (a)   **(1 mark)**

(Your answer must not exceed 5 words)

        (b)   **(1 mark)**

(Total for part (c) : 5 marks)

(Question total : 16 marks)

Question 8

The following diagram shows the cost and revenue curves for a single firm.

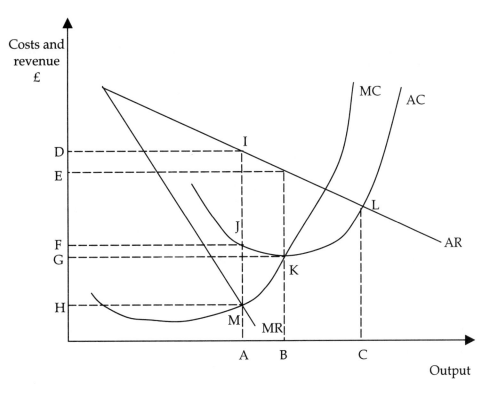

Required

(a) Using your knowledge of economic theory and the diagram above, state what the following are:

    (i)   the equilibrium price

        (1 mark)

    (ii)   the equilibrium output

        (1 mark)

    (iii)   the excess profit

        (1 mark)

        (Total for part (a) : 3 marks)

(b) State the effect of a rise in the firm's costs at all levels of output on

    (i)   the equilibrium price

        (1 mark)

    (ii)   the equilibrium output

        (1 mark)

(iii)   total profits

(1 mark)

(Total for part (b) : 3 marks)

(c)   State what would happen to the firm's average and marginal revenue curves, and its equilibrium price and output, if:

		Effect on AR and MR curves	*Effect on equilibrium price and output*
(i)	*consumer incomes rose*		
		(1 mark)	(1 mark)
(ii)	*new firms enter the industry*		
		(1 mark)	(1 mark)

(Total for part (c) : 4 marks)

(d)   (i)   Explain what the term 'barriers to entry' means.

(Your answer must not exceed 20 words)

(2 marks)

(ii)   Give four examples of barriers to entry.

(Each answer must not exceed 10 words)

(a)   (1 mark)

(b)   (1 mark)

(c)   (1 mark)

(d)   (1 mark)

(Total for part (d) : 6 marks)

(Question total : 16 marks)

Question 9

The following diagram shows the circular flow of income for the UK economy.

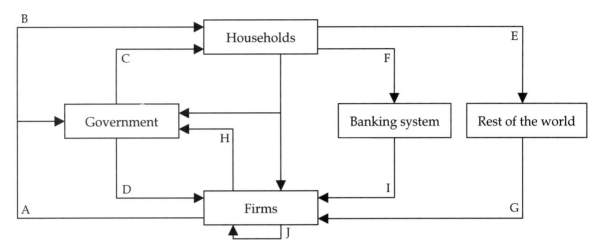

Required

(a)   Using your knowledge of economic theory and the diagram above, state which of the lettered flows in the diagram refer to:

    (i)   a government purchase of computer equipment from a UK producer

                              (1 mark)

    (ii)   a household's transfer incomes

                              (1 mark)

    (iii)   corporation tax

                              (1 mark)

    (iv)   reinvestments of business profits to finance capital investment

                              (1 mark)

    (v)   a UK firm's sales of goods to a firm in Japan

                              (1 mark)

                          (Total for part (a) : 5 marks)

(b)   For an open economy, state:

    (i)   the three injections into the circular flow

        (a)   **(1 mark)**

        (b)   **(1 mark)**

        (c)   **(1 mark)**

(ii) the three withdrawals (leakages) out of the circular flow:

(a)   **(1 mark)**

(b)   **(1 mark)**

(c)   **(1 mark)**

(Total for part (b) : 6 marks)

(c) Explain one effect on the business sector of an economy of:

(i) an increase in the household savings rate

(Your answer should not exceed 20 words)

(2 marks)

(ii) a rise in the exchange rate for the country's currency

(Your answer should not exceed 20 words)

(2 marks)

(Total for part (c) : 4 marks)

(d) Complete the following definition.

Marginal propensity to consume is.....

(Your answer must not exceed 15 words)

(1 mark)

(Total for part (d) : 1 marks)

(Question total : 16 marks)

Question 10

The following is a hypothetical example of two economies, Eastland and Westland.

Each country can produce two goods: wheat and coffee. Each country has two units of resource and uses one in the production of wheat and one in the production of coffee.

Tons of output	Coffee	Wheat
Westland	140	70
Eastland	20	60

Required

(a)   Using your knowledge of economic theory and the data given above, state which country has absolute advantage in the production of coffee and wheat.

(2 marks)

(Total for part (a) : 2 marks)

(b)   For each country, calculate the opportunity cost of the production of coffee and wheat.

	Westland	*Eastland*
Coffee		
	(1 mark)	**(1 mark)**
Wheat		
	(1 mark)	**(1 mark)**

(Total for part (b) : 4 marks)

(c)   If the international rate of exchange was 1.5 tons of coffee for 1 ton of wheat, and Westland specialised completely in the production of coffee, calculate:

(i)   the total output of coffee in Westland

(1 mark)

(ii)   the amount of coffee Westland would have to export in order to import 80 tons of wheat

(1 mark)

(Total for part (c) : 2 marks)

(d)   (i)   State the formula for the terms of trade index

(2 marks)

(ii)   Fill in the gaps in the following sentences (1 word for each gap)

There will be a change in the terms of trade if there is a change in the ▭ rate. A depreciation leads to ▭ export prices and ▭ import prices. This implies a ▭ in the terms of trade.

(1 mark for each word)

(Total for part (d) : 6 marks)

(e)   State two factors which explain why countries are internationally competitive in some products and not in others.

(i)   *(Your answer must not exceed 10 words)*

(1 mark)

(ii)   *(Your answer must not exceed 10 words)*

(1 mark)

(Total for part (e) : 2 marks)

(Question total : 16 marks)

Question 11

The following refers to selected data from a taxation system.

Table A   Government budget for 2003/2004

	£bn
Total expenditure	349
Total receipts	346
of which:	
Income	88
Social security contributions	56
Corporation tax	30
Value added tax	54
Excise duties	36
Business rates	16
Council Tax	13
Other	53

Figure 1   Income and tax

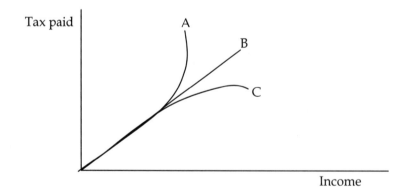

Required

(a)   Using your knowledge of economic theory and the information and diagrams above, complete the following statements defining direct and indirect taxes and, from table A above, give two examples of each.

(i)   Direct taxes are taxes which……..

(Your answer must not exceed 20 words)

(2 marks)

(ii)   Indirect taxes are taxes which………..

(Your answer must not exceed 20 words)

(2 marks)

(iii)   An example of a direct tax is…

(Your answer must not exceed 5 words)

(1 mark)

(iv)   An example of an indirect tax is……

(Your answer must not exceed 5 words)

(1 mark)

(Total for part (a) : 6 marks)

(b)   (i)   From Figure 1 above, state which curve shows:

(a)   a progressive tax   **(1 mark)**

(b)   a regressive tax   **(1 mark)**

(ii)   From Table A above give one example of a progressive tax and one example of a regressive tax.

(a)   Progressive tax   **(1 mark)**

(b)   Regressive tax   **(1 mark)**

(Total for part (b) : 4 marks)

(Question total : 10 marks)

Question 12

(a)   Sketch a diagram to show how the burden of an indirect tax is shared between the business producing the good and the customer.

(2 marks)

(Total for part (a) : 2 marks)

(b)   The Laffer curve

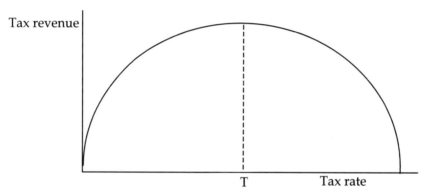

In the diagram above, the Laffer curve shows that if the rate of tax exceeds point T, total revenue received begins to fall. State two reasons to explain this.

(i)   *(Your answer must not exceed 20 words)*

(1 mark)

(ii)   *(Your answer must not exceed 20 words)*

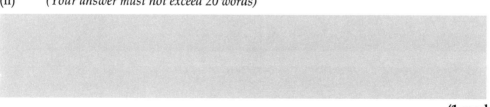

(1 mark)

(Total for part (b) : 2 marks)

(c)   Complete the following statement by giving one reason how a service sector business would be affected if the government reduced taxation by cutting the rate of income tax.

A service sector business will be affected by a cut in income tax, since this will raise the disposable income of customers. This will.........................

(Your answer must not exceed 20 words)

(2 marks)

(Total for part (c) : 2 marks)

(Question total : 6 marks)

Question 13

The following diagram is known as the economic diamond and is used to illustrate how well an economy is performing in terms of the major objectives of economic policy.

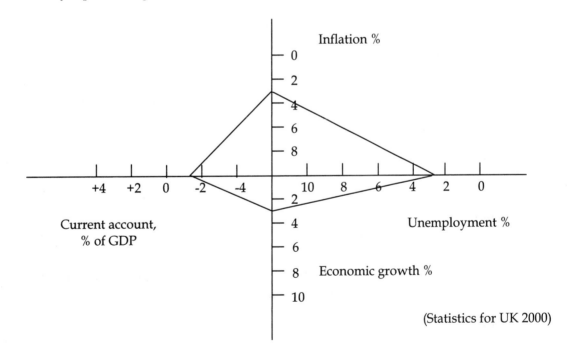

(Statistics for UK 2000)

(a)   Using your knowledge of economic theory and the diagram above, define the following terms.

(Your answers must not exceed 10 words in each case)

(i)   Inflation

(1 mark)

(ii)   Unemployment

(1 mark)

(iii)   Economic growth

(1 mark)

(iv)   Current account

(1 mark)

(Total for part (a) : 4 marks)

(b)   Fill in the gaps in the following sentences (one word for each gap).

If a country improved its overall economic performance, the economic diamond would become _____ . There would be a(n) _____ in all or most of the economic indicators.

(1 mark for each word)

(Total for part(b) : 2 marks)

(c)   State three types of unemployment.

(i)   _____ **(1 mark)**

(ii)   _____ **(1 mark)**

(iii)   _____ **(1 mark)**

(Total for part (c) : 3 marks)

(d)   Unemployment is measured in the UK using two different measures. State what each of these measures is, and briefly explain how each is calculated.

(i)   *(Your explanation must not exceed 20 words)*

(2 marks)

(ii)   *(Your explanation must not exceed 20 words)*

(2 marks)

(Total for part (d) : 4 marks)

(e)   State whether each of the following statements is true or false.

	Encircle your answer in each case	
Raising the rate of income tax will reduce unemployment	*True or False*	**(1 mark)**
Raising the rate of unemployment benefit will reduce unemployment	*True or False*	**(1 mark)**
Raising the rate of interest will reduce unemployment	*True or False*	**(1 mark)**

(Total for part (e) : 3 marks)

(Question total : 16 marks)

Question 14

At the end of 2001, there was a crisis brewing in the coffee industry. In October the Association of Coffee Producing Countries (ACPC), which was a 14 member cartel, announced that it was closing. The cartel could not prevent the breakdown of the export retention scheme in April 2001. In an attempt to halt the continuing decline in wholesale coffee prices, members of the cartel were asked to cut export supply to international markets by 20%. However, quotas were not adhered to and coffee production continued to expand, partly due to Vietnam which was not a member of the cartel but is the second largest coffee producer in the world. Average prices for coffee beans fell throughout 2001, despite both demand and supply increasing.

Required

(a)   Using your knowledge of economic theory and the information given above, fill in the gaps in the following sentence (one word for each gap).

It is obvious why international coffee prices have fallen. Total global
has expanded more rapidly than global   . This has led to a(n)
in coffee stocks and   pressure on price levels.

(1 mark for each word)

(Total for part (a) : 4 marks)

(b)   Draw a diagram with demand and supply curves to show what has happened in the international coffee market in 2001.

(3 marks)

(Total for part (b) : 3 marks)

(c)   (i)   Complete the following statement defining income elasticity of demand:

Income elasticity of demand.....

(Your answer must not exceed 15 words)

(2 marks)

(ii)   State whether you think the income elasticity of demand for high grade coffee is high or low.

(1 mark)

(iii)   Fill in the gap and complete the following statement:

The income elasticity of demand for high grade coffee is   because...

(Your answer must not exceed 20 words)

(2 marks)

(Total for part (c) : 5 marks)

(d)   Because of the substantial fall in coffee prices, many coffee producers are leaving the industry and some are switching to other crops.

(i)   At what output level will a firm decide to leave an industry?

(Your answer must not exceed 10 words)

(2 marks)

(ii)   If suppliers leave the coffee industry, what is likely to happen to the price of coffee?

(Your answer must not exceed 5 words)

(1 mark)

(iii)   Some coffee producers may switch to producing tea. If tea and coffee are substitute goods, what do you know about the cross elasticity of demand between the goods?

(Your answer must not exceed 5 words)

(1 mark)

(Total for part (d) : 4 marks)

(Question total : 16 marks)

Question 15

There have been many instances in the last few years of firms and other organisations polluting their local environment. One example is a water company which polluted the drinking water of a major south coast city.

Incidents such as this are the result of the market mechanism failing to produce the best allocation of resources due to negative externalities. Economists can explain such pollution in terms of the following diagram:

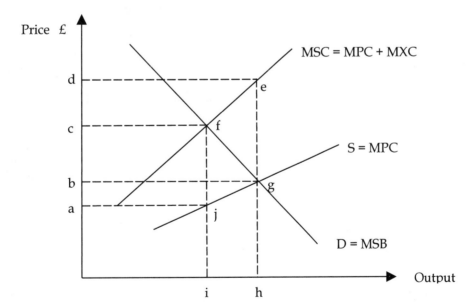

Required

(a)   Using your knowledge of economic theory and the information and diagram given above,

(i)   Complete the following definition of a negative externality.

A negative externality …..

(Your answer must not exceed 15 words)

(2 marks)

(ii)   Give one example of a negative externality.

(Your answer must not exceed 5 words)

(1 mark)

(Total for part (a) : 3 marks)

(b)   With reference to the diagram above, and assuming a competitive market and no government intervention,

(i)   what would be the market equilibrium price and output?

(2 marks)

(ii)   what would be the price and output at the social optimum?

(2 marks)

(iii)   which area signifies the welfare loss as a result of the existence of externalities?

(1 mark)

(Total for part (b) : 5 marks)

(c)   (i)   What is a 'green tax'?

(Your answer must not exceed 15 words)

(2 marks)

(ii)   In order to achieve the socially optimal output, how much would the green tax have to be in the diagram above?

(1 mark)

(Total for part (c) : 3 marks)

(d)   Complete the following statements concerning the MSB and MPC curves, and MXC.

(i)   The MSB curve is also labelled the D curve because.....

(Your answer must not exceed 15 words)

(2 marks)

(ii)   The MPC curve is also labelled the S curve because....

(Your answer must not exceed 15 words)

(2 marks)

(iii)   'MXC' stands for............

(1 mark)
(Total for part (d) : 5 marks)
(Question total : 16 marks)

Question 16

In November 2001 it was announced that UK unemployment figures had risen for the first time in over a year. Ciaran Barr (UK Economist, Deutsche bank) said, 'We are seeing a turning in the labour market. The pressure will stay on the Bank of England to cut interest rates further in the coming months'.

The graph below shows the pattern of UK unemployment from 1988 to 2001, using one of the two accepted measures of unemployment used in the UK.

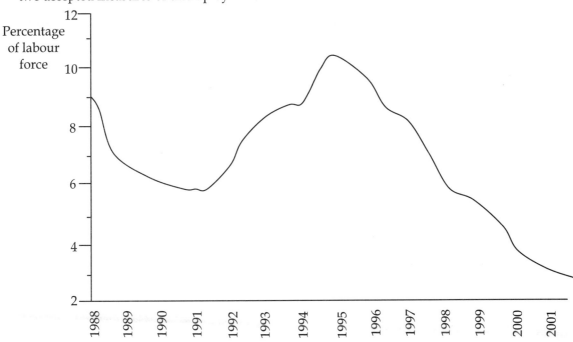

Required

(a)   Using your knowledge of economic theory and the information and diagram given above,

(i)   Name the two measures of unemployment referred to.

(2 marks)

(ii)   Which of the two measures tends to be higher?

(1 mark)

(iii)   Why does this measure tend to be higher?

(Your answer must not exceed 15 words)

(2 marks)

(iv)   Unemployment figures are sometimes quoted as being in seasonally adjusted form.

Complete the following statement explaining what this term means.

(Your answer must not exceed 20 words)

If unemployment figures are quoted as having been seasonally adjusted, this means that they have been…

(2 marks)

(v)   Why is it expected that the Bank of England will cut interest rates following the rise in unemployment?

(Your answer must not exceed 20 words)

(2 marks)

(Total for part (a) : 9 marks)

(b)   State whether each of the following statements is true or false:

	Encircle your answer in each case	
Changing interest rates to affect unemployment is mainly a demand side policy	*True or False*	**(1 mark)**
Making credit more easily available will reduce unemployment	*True or False*	**(1 mark)**
Increasing income tax will reduce unemployment	*True or False*	**(1 mark)**

(Total for part (b) : 3 marks)

(c)   State two types of unemployment, and state the main cause in each case.

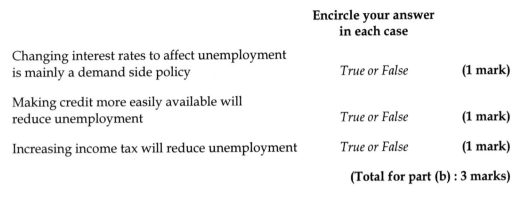

	Type	*Cause*
(i)	**(1 mark)**	**(1 mark)**

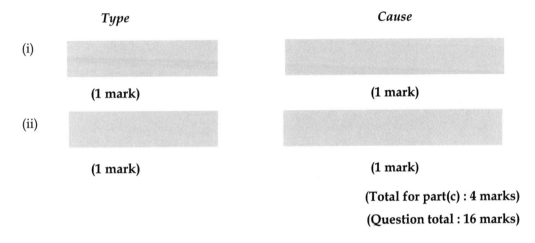

| (ii) | **(1 mark)** | **(1 mark)** |

(Total for part(c) : 4 marks)

(Question total : 16 marks)

Multiple Choice Questions

Question 1

1.1 In all economies, the fundamental economic problem is that:

    (a)   consumers never have as much money as they would wish.

    (b)   resources are scarce relative to human wants.

    (c)   there is always some unemployment of resources.

    (d)   the supply of resources is always less than the demand for them.

(November 1999)

1.2 The 'central economic problem' means:

    (a)   the output of goods and services is limited by scarce resources.

    (b)   market prices do not always equal costs of production.

    (c)   all businesses must make a profit.

    (d)   consumers cannot maximise their utility because of limited information.

(November 1996)

1.3 Which one of the following statements is not true?

    (a)   The basic economic problem is the same in planned and free market economies.

    (b)   The basic economic problem is one of choice between alternatives.

    (c)   Factors of production are limited in supply.

    (d)   Choice is necessary because of limited consumer wants.

(November 1995)

1.4 The 'central economic problem' refers to:

    (a)   the persistence of unemployment.

    (b)   the need to allocate scarce resources between competing uses.

    (c)   consumers having less money than they would like.

    (d)   the need to ensure that in the long run all production costs are covered by sales revenue.

(Pilot Paper 2000)

1.5   The economic problem of what to produce is concerned with:

   (a)   which goods and services and how much of each are to be produced.

   (b)   which goods will meet individual and social needs.

   (c)   which goods will maximise the rate of growth of welfare over time.

   (d)   which combination of resources should be used in production.

(May 2001)

1.6   The opportunity cost of an item or activity is best defined as:

   (a)   the next best item or activity forgone.

   (b)   normal profits.

   (c)   unmeasurable.

   (d)   the return or benefit which could have been derived from the next best item or alternative forgone.

1.7   Which one of the following best describes the opportunity costs to society of building a new school?

   (a)   The increased taxation to pay for the school.

   (b)   The money that was spent on building the school.

   (c)   The other goods that could have been produced with the resources used to build the school.

   (d)   The running cost of the school when it is opened.

(May 1998)

1.8   Which one of the following would shift a country's production possibility frontier (PPF) outwards (to the right)?

   (a)   A fall in unemployment.

   (b)   An increase in exports.

   (c)   A rise in total consumer expenditure.

   (d)   Technical progress reducing production costs.

(Pilot Paper 2000)

1.9 Which of the following would cause the production possibility frontier for an economy to shift outwards?

(i) A reduction in the level of employment.
(ii) A rise in the rate of investment.
(iii) A fall in the price of one factor of production.
(iv) A rise in output per worker.

(a) (i) and (ii) only.

(b) (i), (ii) and (iii) only.

(c) (i), (ii) and (iv) only.

(d) (ii) and (iv) only.

(November 1993)

1.10 The term 'rising economic welfare' refers to:

(a) an increase in state welfare payments.

(b) a rising standard of living.

(c) increased employment opportunities.

(d) increased consumption of health and education services.

(Pilot Paper 2000)

1.11 All of the following government policies would tend to raise the long-term rate of economic growth except which one?

(a) Encouraging a higher level of business investment.

(b) Increasing expenditure on education and training.

(c) Encouraging a higher level of consumer expenditure.

(d) Providing tax relief for research and development expenditure by businesses.

(Pilot Paper 2000)

1.12 Government could raise labour productivity by all of the following except which one?

(a) Providing tax relief for Research and Development expenditure by companies.

(b) Increasing expenditure on education and training.

(c) Reducing discrimination in employment practices.

(d) Reducing social security payments.

(May 2001)

1.13   If an economy experiences an 'increase in productivity', this means that:

   (a)   the level of total output in the economy has risen.

   (b)   employees are working harder than before.

   (c)   output per unit of input has risen.

   (d)   technical change has taken place.

(Pilot Paper 2000)

1.14   Which one of the following is not a factor of production?

   (a)   Unskilled labour.

   (b)   A machine tool.

   (c)   Cash reserves.

   (d)   Entrepreneurship.

(Pilot Paper 2000)

1.15   In economics, normal profit is defined as:

   (a)   the average level of profit earned in an industry.

   (b)   the difference between revenue and costs.

   (c)   the level of profit required to retain entrepreneurs within an industry.

   (d)   the level of profit earned in the long run.

(November 1994)

1.16   Which of the following statements about normal profit are correct?

   (i)   It is the reward for risk taking.
   (ii)   It is the return to entrepreneurship.
   (iii)   It is the cost of entrepreneurship.
   (iv)   It is earned only in the short run.

   (a)   (i) and (ii) only.

   (b)   (ii) and (iii) only.

   (c)   (i), (ii) and (iii) only.

   (d)   (i), (ii) and (iv) only.

(May 1998)

1.17   Which one of the following is a feature of a market economy?

   (a)   Prices are determined mainly by market forces.

   (b)   Resources are allocated between different markets by administrative decisions.

   (c)   Consumer preferences are determined by market research.

   (d)   All markets are characterised by a high degree of competition.

(Pilot Paper 2000)

1.18   In a planned economy:

    (a)   there is a fair allocation of resources.

    (b)   profits are kept to a minimum.

    (c)   directives are used to allocate resources.

    (d)   there is allocative efficiency.

1.19   In a market economy, the allocation of resources between different productive activities is determined mainly by:

    (a)   decisions of the government.

    (b)   wealth of entrepreneurs.

    (c)   pattern of consumer expenditure.

    (d)   supply of factors of production.

(November 1998)

1.20   Which one of the following is not a function of profit in a market economy?

    (a)   A signal to producers.

    (b)   A signal to consumers.

    (c)   The return to entrepreneurship.

    (d)   A reward for risk taking.

(November 1997)

Question 2

2.1   Effective demand is:

    (a)   demand derived from demand for the final product.

    (b)   demand backed by the ability to pay.

    (c)   demand affected by advertising.

    (d)   demand of rich people.

2.2   Which of the following will not cause an increase in the demand for a product?

    (a)   An increase in consumers' incomes.

    (b)   An increase in the price of a rival product.

    (c)   A decrease in the price of a complementary good.

    (d)   An increase in the price of the product.

(FTC Internal Exam June 1998)

2.3   An increase in demand causes an increase in price; therefore, an increase in price will cause an increase in demand. This statement is:

(a)   always false.

(b)   true for normal goods only.

(c)   false for inferior goods only.

(d)   true for all goods.

2.4   Which of the following would not cause a decrease in the demand for a product?

(a)   Advertising of a rival product.

(b)   An increase in the price of a complementary product.

(c)   A decrease in the price of the product.

(d)   A decrease in income tax (assuming the product to be an inferior good).

2.5   Which of the following would NOT bring about a shift outwards of the demand curve for a commodity X?

(a)   An increase in the size of the population.

(b)   A rise in the price of X.

(c)   A successful advertising campaign.

(d)   A fall in the price of a complement for X.

2.6   The demand curve for a good will shift to the right:

(a)   if there is an increase in the supply of the good.

(b)   if the price of the good falls.

(c)   if consumer incomes rise.

(d)   when the price of a substitute good falls.

(November 1997)

2.7   Which one of the following will cause the demand curve for a good to move to the right?

(a)   A decrease in the costs of producing the good.

(b)   A fall in the price of the good.

(c)   An increase in the price of a complementary good.

(d)   An increase in the price of a close substitute good.

(November 1996)

2.8   The demand curve for the product of a business will shift to the right when there is:

    (a)   a reduction in indirect tax on the good.

    (b)   an improvement in production which lowers costs.

    (c)   a fall in the price of the good.

    (d)   an increase in the supply of a complementary good.

(Pilot Paper 2000)

2.9   Which of the following could cause an upward and leftward movement of an upward-sloping supply curve for a commodity?

    (a)   The imposition of an excise tax.

    (b)   A rise in productivity.

    (c)   A fall in production costs.

    (d)   A shift of tastes in favour of the product.

2.10   Which of the following will not cause an increase in supply?

    (a)   A technological advance.

    (b)   New producers entering the market.

    (c)   A reduction in an indirect tax.

    (d)   A decrease in product price.

(FTC Internal Exam June 1999)

2.11   If the price of coffee increases, which one of the following would be expected to occur?

    (a)   A rise in the quantity of coffee demanded.

    (b)   A fall in the demand for tea.

    (c)   A fall in the price of tea.

    (d)   A rise in the demand for tea.

(FTC Internal Exam December 1998)

2.12   If the demand for a good increases, which one of the following will occur?

    (a)   Price rises and the quantity sold falls.

    (b)   Price falls and the quantity sold rises.

    (c)   Price and quantity sold both rise.

    (d)   Price and quantity sold both fall.

(May 2001)

2.13   Products are 'joint products' if:

    (a)   they are necessarily produced by a given process.

    (b)   a consumer will only buy one if he can also buy the other.

    (c)   the products are substitutes.

    (d)   the products are complements.

2.14   Of three goods, A is a substitute for, and B complementary to, a third good C. A rise in the price of C following an increase in the costs of production will cause the demand for:

    (a)   A and C to fall.

    (b)   A to rise and the demand for B to fall.

    (c)   B and C to fall, leaving demand for A unchanged.

    (d)   C to fall, leaving demand for A and B unchanged.

2.15   Consumer surplus is:

    (a)   the difference between the price producers are willing to supply at and the price they actually receive.

    (b)   the difference between the price the consumer is willing to pay and the price he actually pays.

    (c)   the welfare of societies.

    (d)   the excess of profit over normal profit.

2.16   In a free enterprise economy, the price mechanism determines:

    (i)   the allocation of resources between different industries.
    (ii)   the rewards paid to factors of production.
    (iii)   the types of goods and services produced.
    (iv)   the preferences of consumers.

Which one of the above are correct?

    (a)   (i) and (iii) only.

    (b)   (i) and (iv) only.

    (c)   (i), (ii) and (iii) only.

    (d)   (i), (iii) and (iv) only.

(May 1993)

2.17   Other things being equal, if the government fixed a maximum price on a good in order to protect consumers, but this price was above the price prevailing in a free market:

   (a)   suppliers would increase their prices.

   (b)   the demand for the good would fall.

   (c)   output would increase.

   (d)   none of the above.

2.18   If the government sets a maximum rent which landlords can charge for private rented accommodation, which is a little below the rent which would prevail in a free market, which of the following is likely to happen?

   (i)   Increased demand for council accommodation.
   (ii)   Lots of houses standing empty.

   (a)   (i) and (ii).

   (b)   (i) only.

   (c)   (ii) only.

   (d)   Neither (i) nor (ii).

2.19   The demand for and supply of a good are in equilibrium. An indirect tax is levied on the good. Which one of the following will show the new equilibrium?

   (a)   A shift in the supply curve to the right.

   (b)   A shift in the demand curve to the right.

   (c)   A shift in the supply curve to the left.

   (d)   A shift in the demand curve to the left.

(November 1995)

2.20   Indirect taxes are:

   (a)   levied on income.

   (b)   not paid directly.

   (c)   levied on expenditure.

   (d)   always ad valorem taxes.

Question 3

3.1   If the demand for a firm's product has a price elasticity of –2, a 10% fall in its price will:

   (a)   decrease total revenue by 20%.

   (b)   increase sales volume by 10%.

   (c)   increase sales volume by 20%.

   (d)   increase total revenue by 20%.

(Pilot Paper 2000)

3.2   If the demand for a good is price inelastic, then the total expenditure on the good:

(a)   will fall if the price rises.

(b)   will be constant if the price rises.

(c)   will rise if the price rises.

(d)   will rise if the price falls.

(November 1999)

3.3   If the demand for a good is price elastic, which one of the following is true?

When the price of the good:

(a)   rises, the quantity demanded falls and total expenditure on the good increases.

(b)   rises, the quantity demanded falls and total expenditure on the good decreases.

(c)   falls, the quantity demanded rises and total expenditure on the good decreases.

(d)   falls, the quantity demanded rises and total expenditure on the good is unchanged.

(November 1998)

3.4   When only a small proportion of a consumers' income is spent on a good:

(a)   the demand for the good will be highly price elastic.

(b)   the good is described as 'inferior'.

(c)   a rise in the price of the good will strongly encourage a search for substitutes.

(d)   the demand for the good will be price inelastic.

(November 1996)

3.5   If the demand for a good is price inelastic, which one of the following statements is correct?

(a)   If the price of the good rises, the total revenue earned by the producer of the good increases.

(b)   If the price of the good rises, the total revenue earned by the producer of the good falls.

(c)   If the price of the good falls, the total revenue earned by the producer increases.

(d)   If the price of the good falls, the total revenue earned by the producer is unaffected.

(May 1996)

3.6   If the price elasticity of demand for a product is less than one then a firm can increase its profits:

   (a)   by increasing its price.

   (b)   by decreasing its price.

   (c)   by advertising to develop brand loyalty.

   (d)   it is impossible to tell whether profits can be increased without further information.

3.7   A business currently selling 10,000 units of its product per month plans to reduce the retail price from £1 to £0.90. It knows from experience that the price elasticity of demand for this product is –1.5.

   Assuming no other changes, the sales which the business can now expect will be:

   (a)   8,500

   (b)   9,000

   (c)   11,000

   (d)   11,500

(Specimen 1994/5)

3.8   If the demand for a good is price elastic, a fall in price will lead to:

   (i)   a rise in sales.
   (ii)   a fall in sales.
   (iii)   a rise in total expenditure on the good.
   (iv)   a fall in total expenditure on the good.

   (a)   (i) and (iii) only.

   (b)   (i) and (iv) only.

   (c)   (ii) and (iii) only.

   (d)   (ii) and (iv) only.

(May 1995)

3.9   If the price elasticity of demand for a product is greater than one then a firm can increase its profits:

   (a)   by increasing its price.

   (b)   by decreasing its price.

   (c)   by advertising to develop brand loyalty.

   (d)   it is impossible to tell whether profits can be increased without further information.

3.10   If the price elasticity of demand for a product is greater than one, which one of the following statements is correct?

   (a)   If the price of the good increases, the total revenue earned by the firm decreases.

   (b)   If the price of the good increases, the total revenue earned by the firm remains constant.

   (c)   If the price of the good increases, the total revenue earned by the firm increases.

   (d)   If the price of the good decreases, the total revenue earned by the firm decreases.

(FTC Internal Exam June 1998)

3.11   The demand for a product will tend to be elastic when:

   (a)   it is habit forming.

   (b)   it has many close substitutes.

   (c)   it is relatively cheap.

   (d)   it is a basic necessity.

(FTC Internal Exam December 1998)

3.12   When the price elasticity of demand for a product is less than one:

   (a)   a fall in price leads to an increase in expenditure.

   (b)   an increase in price leads to a fall in expenditure.

   (c)   a fall in price leads to a decrease in expenditure.

   (d)   an increase in price could increase or decrease expenditure.

(FTC Internal Exam December 1999)

3.13   A shift to the right in the supply curve of a good, the demand remaining unchanged, will reduce its price to a greater degree:

   (a)   the more elastic the demand curve.

   (b)   the less elastic the demand curve.

   (c)   the nearer the elasticity of demand to unity.

   (d)   the more elastic the supply curve.

(May 1996)

3.14   Which one of the following statements about the elasticity of supply is not true?

   (a)   It tends to vary with time.

   (b)   It is a measure of the responsiveness of supply to changes in price.

   (c)   It is a measure of changes in supply due to greater efficiency.

   (d)   It tends to be higher for manufactured goods than for primary products.

(November 1995)

3.15   Which one of the following will produce the largest fluctuations in a market price?

(a)   Large shifts in supply with price elastic demand.

(b)   Large shifts in supply with price inelastic demand.

(c)   Large shifts in supply with perfectly price elastic demand.

(d)   Small shifts in supply with price inelastic demand.

(May 2001)

3.16   If the cross elasticity of demand between two goods is +1.125, this implies:

(a)   that the goods are substitutes.

(b)   that demand is relatively elastic.

(c)   that the goods are complements.

(d)   that the goods are both normal goods.

(FTC Internal Exam June 1998)

3.17   If the cross elasticity of demand between two goods is –0.75, this implies:

(a)   the goods are complements.

(b)   demand is relatively inelastic.

(c)   the goods are both inferior goods.

(d)   the goods are substitutes.

(FTC Internal Exam June 1999)

3.18   The imposition of an indirect tax on a good with a given elasticity of supply will have the most effect on market price when:

(a)   demand is relatively price elastic.

(b)   price elasticity of demand is equal to unity.

(c)   demand is relatively price inelastic.

(d)   price elasticity tends towards infinity.

(May 1994)

3.19   An indirect tax is imposed on a consumer good. Which combination of price elasticities of supply and demand will lead to the burden of tax being greater for the consumers than for the producers of the good?

(a)   Inelastic demand, inelastic supply.

(b)   Inelastic demand, elastic supply.

(c)   Elastic demand, inelastic supply.

(d)   Elastic demand, elastic supply.

3.20   An inferior good is one which has an income elasticity of demand that is:

(a)   positive but less than unity.

(b)   negative.

(c)   unity.

(d)   zero.

(May 1994)

Question 4

4.1   Which one of the following is not a cost of production to the firm?

(a)   Salaries of senior managers.

(b)   Normal profit.

(c)   Interest payable on loans.

(d)   Corporation tax.

(November 1999)

4.2   Which one of the following would be a variable cost to a firm?

(a)   Mortgage payments on the factory.

(b)   The cost of raw materials.

(c)   Depreciation of machines owing to age.

(d)   Interest on debentures.

(May 1997)

4.3   A firm's total fixed costs are £1,200. At a certain output level its average total costs per unit are £10 and the average variable cost per unit is £7. That level of output is:

(a)   200 units.

(b)   300 units.

(c)   400 units.

(d)   500 units.

4.4   The short-run average-cost curve for firms rises after a certain level of output because of:

(a)   diseconomies of scale.

(b)   the law of diminishing returns.

(c)   diminishing marginal utility.

(d)   rising price of factors of production.

(Pilot Paper 2000)

4.5   By the U-shaped cost curve is meant the tendency for:

    (a)   average fixed costs to fall at first and then rise.

    (b)   marginal costs to rise at first and then fall.

    (c)   total costs to fall at first and then rise.

    (d)   average total costs to fall at first and then rise.

4.6   The long run average cost curve for a business will eventually rise because of:

    (a)   the law of diminishing returns.

    (b)   increasing competition in the industry.

    (c)   limits to the size of the market for the good.

    (d)   diseconomies of scale.

(November 1998)

4.7   If average variable costs are increasing:

    (a)   average variable costs must exceed marginal costs.

    (b)   marginal costs must exceed average variable costs.

    (c)   a firm is earning less than normal profits.

    (d)   average total costs must be increasing.

4.8   Marginal cost is best defined as:

    (a)   the difference between total fixed costs and total variable costs.

    (b)   costs which are too small to influence prices.

    (c)   the change in total costs when output rises by one unit.

    (d)   fixed costs per unit of output.

(November 1996)

4.9   When average cost is falling, marginal cost:

    (a)   must be falling faster than average cost.

    (b)   must be less than average cost.

    (c)   may be greater than, less than or equal to average cost.

    (d)   must be greater than average cost.

4.10   Marginal cost is:

(a)   the average variable cost of production.

(b)   the change in total cost when output rises by one unit.

(c)   total cost minus total fixed cost.

(d)   the average cost of the last unit produced.

(November 1993)

4.11   Which of the following statements about the short run marginal cost curve is NOT true?

(a)   When average cost is falling, marginal cost will be below average cost.

(b)   Marginal cost is greater than average cost when the number of units produced is greater than the optimum technical output.

(c)   Marginal cost will be rising under conditions of diminishing returns.

(d)   Marginal cost is unaffected by changes in factor prices.

4.12   Which of the following always rise when a manufacturing business increases its output?

(i)   Fixed cost.
(ii)   Marginal cost.
(iii)   Average variable cost.
(iv)   Total costs.

(a)   (i) and (ii) only.

(b)   (ii) and (iii) only.

(c)   (iii) and (iv) only.

(d)   (iv) only.

(November 1998)

4.13   If the total cost curve of a firm is an upward sloping straight line through the origin:

(a)   average costs are rising, but marginal costs may be rising or falling.

(b)   marginal and average costs are rising.

(c)   fixed costs are zero.

(d)   price elasticity of supply is equal to 1.

4.14   The 'law of diminishing returns' can apply to a business only when:

(a)   all factors of production can be varied.

(b)   at least one factor of production is fixed.

(c)   all factors of production are fixed.

(d)   capital used in production is fixed.

(May 1998)

4.15   Decreasing returns to scale can only occur:

(a)   in the short run.

(b)   in the long run.

(c)   if there is one fixed factor of production.

(d)   if companies have monopoly power.

(November 1996)

4.16   The law of diminishing returns explains:

(a)   why diseconomies of scale exist.

(b)   why demand curves slope downwards from left to right.

(c)   the shape of a firm's short run cost curves.

(d)   the importance of negative externalities.

(FTC Internal Exam June 1998)

4.17   The law of diminishing returns:

(a)   is based on economies of scale.

(b)   usually relates to short run productivity and costs.

(c)   depends on diseconomies of scale.

(d)   explains falling marginal utility from consumption of a good.

(FTC Internal Exam December 1999)

4.18   Economies of scale:

(a)   can be gained only by monopoly firms.

(b)   are possible only if there is a sufficient demand for the product.

(c)   do not necessarily reduce unit costs of production.

(d)   depend on the efficiency of management.

(May 1996)

4.19   Which of the following are external economies of scale for a business enterprise?

(i)   A locally available trained labour force.
(ii)   The presence of specialist firms providing components.
(iii)   The ability of larger firms to secure cheaper bank loans.
(iv)   The development of specialised transport and communications facilities.

(a)   (i), (ii) and (iii) only.

(b)   (ii), (iii) and (iv) only.

(c)   (i), (ii) and (iv) only.

(d)   (i), (iii) and (iv) only.

(November 1994)

4.20   Diseconomies of scale occur in a business when:

(a)   minimum efficient scale is reached.

(b)   short run variable costs begin to rise.

(c)   x-inefficiency exists.

(d)   long run average costs begin to rise.

(May 2001)

Question 5

5.1   What is the normal profit per unit of a product?

(a)   The difference between its average revenue and average cost.

(b)   The difference between its marginal revenue and marginal cost.

(c)   An element in the average total cost of producing the product.

(d)   The profit per unit that should be earned under normal trading conditions in any market.

5.2   A firm will earn sufficient revenue to cover normal profit if it operates at a position where:

(a)   marginal revenue equals marginal cost.

(b)   demand equals supply.

(c)   price equals average total cost.

(d)   average revenue equals average variable cost.

5.3   A firm will leave the market immediately if:

(a)   average revenue is less than average total costs.

(b)   fixed costs are more than variable costs.

(c)   average revenue is less than average fixed costs.

(d)   average revenue is less than average variable costs.

5.4   A firm operating in the short run will cease production once price falls below that point where revenue equals:

(a)   total costs.

(b)   variable costs.

(c)   fixed costs.

(d)   unavoidable costs.

5.5   Firms are productively efficient when they produce at:

(a)   the lowest point on the average fixed cost curve.

(b)   the output level where total costs are minimised.

(c)   the lowest point on the marginal cost curve.

(d)   the lowest point on the average cost curve.

5.6   Dynamic efficiency:

(a)   results from improvements in productive or technical efficiency which occur over time.

(b)   occurs when price equals marginal cost.

(c)   results from the business moving to a different location.

(d)   is more important than static efficiency.

5.7   When an entrepreneur is maximising his profits, which of the following will be found not to be true?

(a)   The average revenue curve will be elastic.

(b)   Marginal revenue will be positive.

(c)   The average cost curve will inevitably be at its lowest point.

(d)   The average revenue curve will indicate the price charged.

5.8   Which of the following schedules is/are necessary to determine a firm's optimum output in terms of efficiency?

(i)   Average variable cost.
(ii)   Marginal revenue.
(iii) Average total cost.
(iv)   Marginal cost.

(a)   (ii) and (iv) only.

(b)   (i) and (iv) only.

(c)   (iii) only.

(d)   (i) only.

5.9   The breakeven output for a firm is that at which:

(a)   marginal cost = marginal revenue.

(b)   marginal cost = average cost.

(c)   marginal revenue = average cost.

(d)   average cost = average revenue.

5.10   When price is constant:

(a)   total revenue is not a straight line.

(b)   average revenue equals marginal revenue.

(c)   it is impossible for the firm to make a loss.

(d)   average revenue equals average cost.

5.11   Allocative efficiency occurs at the output level where:

(a)   price equals marginal cost.

(b)   price equals average cost.

(c)   average cost is at a minimum.

(d)   marginal cost equals marginal revenue.

5.12   Abnormal profit:

(a)   is the excess of profit over and above normal profit.

(b)   is unusual.

(c)   is only earned by monopolies.

(d)   is only earned in the short run.

5.13   If average revenue is a straight line and slopes downwards:

(a)   marginal revenue will be horizontal.

(b)   marginal revenue will be a constant.

(c)   marginal revenue will slope down and be equal to average revenue.

(d)   marginal revenue will slope down at twice the gradient of the average revenue curve.

5.14   If a firm wishes to maximise its sales revenue, it will produce at the output level where:

(a)   marginal revenue is positive.

(b)   average revenue is at its maximum.

(c)   output is at a maximum.

(d)   marginal revenue is zero.

5.15   A loss making firm will remain in the market in the short run if its total revenue at least covers:

(a)   fixed costs.

(b)   variable costs.

(c)   total costs.

(d)   normal profits.

5.16   Long run abnormal profits can be earned in an industry provided:

(a)   the entry of new firms to the industry is restricted.

(b)   firms can produce at the profit-maximising level of output.

(c)   firms can use the most efficient production methods.

(d)   the demand for the good is price elastic.

(May 1995)

5.17   At the output level where total revenue is maximised:

(a)   marginal revenue = 1.

(b)   marginal revenue is minimised.

(c)   marginal revenue is zero.

(d)   marginal revenue is maximised.

5.18   The minimum price needed for a firm to remain in production in the short run is equal to:

(a)   average fixed cost.

(b)   average variable cost.

(c)   average total cost.

(d)   marginal cost.

5.19   A profit maximising firm will attempt to produce where:

(a)   marginal cost is equal to marginal revenue.

(b)   average costs of production are lowest.

(c)   marginal cost equals average costs.

(d)   marginal cost is equal to average revenue.

(November 1999)

5.20   Which of the following is not consistent with short run profit maximisation?

(a)   Marginal revenue exceeds marginal costs.

(b)   Average revenue equals price.

(c)   Average revenue exceeds average costs.

(d)   Marginal revenue equals marginal costs.

(FTC Internal Exam December 1998)

Question 6

6.1   In perfect competition, when a firm is in short run equilibrium, which of the following must be true?

   (i)   Marginal cost must equal marginal revenue.
   (ii)   Average cost must equal average revenue.
   (iii)   Marginal revenue must equal average revenue.
   (iv)   Marginal cost must equal average cost.

   (a)   (i) and (ii) only.

   (b)   (i) and (iii) only.

   (c)   (ii) and (iii) only.

   (d)   All of them.

6.2   Which of the following describes the possible pricing patterns of firms in perfect competition?

   (a)   Each firm charges a different price to allow for different transport costs.

   (b)   Firms may sell at a higher price than minimum average costs in the short run.

   (c)   Firms may charge less than minimum average costs in the long run.

   (d)   Firms may charge less than average fixed costs in the long run.

6.3   The average revenue curve of a firm in perfect competition is:

   (a)   U-shaped.

   (b)   L-shaped.

   (c)   parallel to the x axis.

   (d)   parallel to the y axis.

6.4   In a perfectly competitive market:

   (a)   a firm's supply curve is its marginal cost curve above average variable cost.

   (b)   a firm's demand curve is perfectly inelastic.

   (c)   firms always make normal profits.

   (d)   firms break even in the long run.

                                                        (FTC Internal Exam December 1999)

6.5   A single firm operating under conditions of perfect competition wishes to maximise profits. It should produce the output level where:

(i)   price equals marginal costs.
(ii)   price exceeds marginal revenue.
(iii)   marginal revenue equals marginal costs.

Which of the following is correct?

(a)   (i) only.

(b)   (iii) only.

(c)   (ii) and (iii) only.

(d)   (i) and (iii) only.

6.6   Which one of the following comes closest to the model of a perfectly competitive industry?

(a)   Oil refining.

(b)   Agriculture.

(c)   Motor vehicles.

(d)   Banking.

(November 1997)

6.7   In a perfectly competitive market, all producers charge the same price because:

(a)   they are all profit maximisers.

(b)   they have the same costs.

(c)   the product is homogeneous.

(d)   all firms are small.

(November 1998)

6.8   Which of the following best describes the condition known as monopsony?

(a)   A market has only one consumer.

(b)   A market has only one supplier.

(c)   A market is regulated by central or local government to ensure a uniform price.

(d)   A single product is traded in the market.

6.9   Which of the following is a necessary condition for a firm to practise price discrimination between two markets?

(a)   The firm has different production costs in the two separated markets.

(b)   The elasticities of demand are different in the two separated markets.

(c)   Consumers are unaware of the price difference between the two separated markets.

(d)   There are no costs involved in separating the two markets.

6.10   A profit maximising price discriminator charges higher prices:

(a)   where demand is less elastic.

(b)   where there is more demand.

(c)   where costs are higher.

(d)   where there is a higher elasticity of demand.

(FTC Internal Exam June 1999)

6.11   The conditions necessary for a successful policy of price discrimination by a company include which of the following?

(i)   There are at least two separate markets.
(ii)   Marginal costs are different in each market.
(iii)   The price elasticities of demand are different in each market.
(iv)   The price elasticities of demand are the same in each market.

(a)   (i) and (ii) only.

(b)   (i) and (iii) only.

(c)   (i), (ii) and (iii) only.

(d)   (ii) and (iv) only.

November 1996

6.12   Which one of the following is an example of price discrimination?

(a)   A bus company charging a lower price than a railway company for the same distance travelled.

(b)   A telecommunications company charging reduced rates for telephone calls made by government bodies.

(c)   Supermarkets charging different prices for fruit in different regions because local supply costs vary.

(d)   Petrol stations charging lower prices for unleaded petrol than for leaded petrol.

(November 1999)

6.13   When a monopolist is maximising his profits, which of the following will be found not to be true?

   (a)   The average revenue curve will be elastic.

   (b)   Marginal revenue will be positive.

   (c)   The average cost curve will inevitably be at its lowest point.

   (d)   The average revenue curve will indicate the price charged.

6.14   Which of the following are likely to confirm the presence of monopoly power in a market?

   (i)   An industrial concentration ratio whereby the three largest firms account for 80% of sales.

   (ii)   Firms are producing where the average revenue exceeds the marginal cost of production.

   (iii) All firms are producing at less than optimum output.

   (a)   (i) only.

   (b)   (i) and (ii) only.

   (c)   (i), (ii) and (iii) only.

   (d)   (ii) and (iii).

(Specimen 1994/95)

6.15   Which of the following does not act as a barrier to entry into an industry?

   (a)   Internal economies of scale.

   (b)   External economies of scale.

   (c)   High start up costs.

   (d)   The threat of a price war.

(FTC Internal Exam December 1999)

6.16   Which one of the following would not act as a barrier to the entry of new firms into an industry?

   (a)   Perfect consumer knowledge.

   (b)   Economies of scale.

   (c)   High fixed costs of production.

   (d)   Brand loyalty.

(May 1997)

6.17   Which one of the following will tend to increase competition within an industry?

   (a)   Economies of scale.

   (b)   Barriers to entry.

   (c)   Low fixed costs.

   (d)   Limited consumer knowledge.

(November 1997)

6.18   Which one of the following will tend to increase the degree of competition in an industry?

   (a)   Product differentiation.

   (b)   Horizontal integration.

   (c)   Economies of scale.

   (d)   Low fixed costs.

(Pilot Paper 2000)

6.19   According to the traditional theory of the firm, the equilibrium position for all firms will be where:

   (a)   profits are maximised.

   (b)   output is maximised.

   (c)   revenue is maximised.

   (d)   costs are minimised.

(May 1998)

6.20   Opportunity cost is:

   (a)   the lowest marginal cost of a product.

   (b)   the difference between fixed and variable costs.

   (c)   the loss of the next best alternative.

   (d)   equal to average variable cost in perfect competition.

(FTC Internal Exam December 1999)

Question 7

7.1   In oligopolistic industries, interdependence of decision-making arises because:

   (a)   the effect of decisions by one firm depends on the reactions of others.

   (b)   there is heavy advertising of products.

   (c)   firms always find it more profitable to collude than to compete.

   (d)   the reaction of rival firms is uncertain.

(Pilot Paper 2000)

7.2   All of the following are characteristics of oligopolies except which one?

(a)   There is a small number of firms in the industry.

(b)   There is a preference for non-price competition.

(c)   There is very little product differentiation.

(d)   There are entry barriers to the industry.

(November 1999)

7.3   Which of the following is not normally a characteristic of an oligopolistic market?

(a)   Heavy expenditure on advertising.

(b)   Abnormal profits in the long run.

(c)   Barriers to the entry of new firms.

(d)   Severe price competition.

(Specimen 1994/5)

7.4   Which one of the following would not normally be a feature of an oligopolistic market?

(a)   Competition through product differentiation.

(b)   The creation of barriers to entry.

(c)   Competition through price wars.

(d)   A tendency for producers to collude.

(November 1994)

7.5   Which of the following statements concerning oligopoly is incorrect?

(a)   A few firms dominate the market.

(b)   Products are usually differentiated.

(c)   Firms can make long run super-normal profits.

(d)   There is usually a high degree of price competition.

(FTC Internal Exam December 1998)

7.6   The kinked demand curve model of oligopoly is designed to explain:

(a)   price leadership.

(b)   price rigidity.

(c)   collusion between producers.

(d)   price competition.

(May 2001)

7.7   Which of the following are common features of oligopolistic industries?

        (i)   A small number of companies.
        (ii)   Barriers to entry.
        (iii)   Product differentiation.
        (iv)   The absence of long run excess profits.

        (a)   (i), (ii) and (iii) only.

        (b)   (ii), (iii) and (iv) only.

        (c)   (i), (ii) and (iv) only.

        (d)   (i), (iii) and (iv) only.

(November 1997)

7.8   Which of the following are characteristics of monopolistic competition?

        (i)   Freedom of entry into the industry.
        (ii)   Homogeneous products.
        (iii)   Advertising.
        (iv)   A downward sloping demand curve.

        (a)   (i) and (ii) only.

        (b)   (i) and (iv) only.

        (c)   (i), (iii) and (iv) only.

        (d)   (ii) and (iv) only.

(May 1996)

7.9   Which of the following statements is true under conditions of monopolistic competition?

        (a)   Each firm fixes its price irrespective of other firms.

        (b)   There is no freedom of entry into the industry in the long run.

        (c)   Buyers and sellers have perfect information.

        (d)   Firms tend to rely heavily on product differentiation.

(May 1995)

7.10   Which one of the following conditions is not a characteristic of monopolistic competition?

        (a)   There are many buyers and sellers in the market.

        (b)   Demand is infinitely elastic.

        (c)   Marginal revenue is less than average revenue.

        (d)   Marginal cost is equal to marginal revenue at the point of profit maximisation.

(November 1995)

7.11   Under monopolistic competition, excess profits are eliminated in the long run because of:

(a)   the lack of barriers to entry.

(b)   the effects of product differentiation.

(c)   the existence of excess capacity.

(d)   the downward sloping demand curve for the product.

(May 2001)

7.12   The benefits to a company when it locates close to other companies in the same industry include all of the following except which one?

(a)   The benefits of bulk buying.

(b)   The provision of specialist commercial services.

(c)   The development of dedicated transport and marketing facilities.

(d)   The supply of labour with relevant skills.

(November 1998)

7.13   All of the following would lead firms in an industry to locate close together in one area except which one?

(a)   A local supply of raw materials.

(b)   Specialist training facilities located in the area.

(c)   The opportunity of external economies of scale.

(d)   The existence of a cartel in the industry.

(November 1999)

7.14   The purpose of a cartel is to:

(a)   rationalise production.

(b)   reduce consumer uncertainty.

(c)   standardise product quality.

(d)   ensure that all producers charge the same price.

(May 1996)

7.15   Vertical integration means:

(a)   a merger between two competing firms in the same industry.

(b)   the takeover by firm X of the suppliers to firm Y.

(c)   the establishment of a cartel to maintain price levels.

(d)   the combination of a firm with its suppliers or customers in the chain of production.

(May 1995)

7.16   A horizontal merger involves:

(a)   the acquisition of a potential customer.

(b)   the acquisition of a potential supplier.

(c)   the acquisition of a potential competitor.

(d)   growth by diversification.

(FTC Internal Exam December 1999)

7.17   Under monopoly and imperfect competition:

(a)   price is equal to marginal revenue.

(b)   price is above marginal revenue.

(c)   price is above average revenue.

(d)   price is below marginal revenue.

(FTC Internal Exam June 1998)

7.18

Quantity (Q)	Total Revenue (TR)	Marginal Revenue (MR)	Average Revenue (AR)
1	£1.00	£1.00	£1.00
2	£1.50	£0.50	£0.75
3	£1.80	£0.30	£0.60

Which market structure could never be consistent with the above table?

(a)   Monopoly.

(b)   Perfect competition.

(c)   Oligopoly.

(d)   Monopolistic competition.

7.19   The long run equilibrium output of a firm will always be where average cost is lowest when the firm is:

(a)   a monopolist.

(b)   an oligopolist.

(c)   a firm in monopolistic competition.

(d)   a firm in perfect competition.

(November 1994)

7.20   Small firms will be most common in an industry when:

    (i)   the market for the product is dispersed.
    (ii)   advertising and brand loyalty is important.
    (iii)   research expenditure is necessary to keep products up to date.
    (iv)   production is characterised by constant returns to scale.

    (a)   (i) and (ii) only.

    (b)   (i), (ii) and (iii) only.

    (c)   (i) and (iv) only.

    (d)   (ii), (iii) and (iv) only.

(November 1993)

Question 8

8.1   Which of the following would cause a firm's demand curve for labour to shift to the right?

    (a)   A rise in the price of the firm's product.

    (b)   A fall in the level of wages.

    (c)   An increase in the supply of labour.

    (d)   A fall in output per worker.

(November 1993)

8.2   All of the following would lead to an upward shift in a firm's demand curve for labour except which one?

    (a)   An increase in the demand for the firm's product.

    (b)   An increase in the productivity of labour.

    (c)   A fall in the price of labour.

    (d)   A rise in the price of substitute factors of production.

(May 2001)

8.3   A business employs 11 workers at a wage of £24 per day. To attract one more worker it raises the wages to £25 per day.

The marginal cost of employing the extra worker is:

    (a)   £1

    (b)   £12

    (c)   £25

    (d)   £36

(May 1995)

8.4   Jones gets a higher wage than Smith because he spent far longer in training.

        As an explanation of wage differentials this statement is:

        (a)   satisfactory, since Jones is entitled to compensation for the income foregone during this training period.

        (b)   satisfactory, since Jones will be more skilled than Smith.

        (c)   unsatisfactory, since it only deals with factors which affect demand.

        (d)   unsatisfactory, since it only deals with factors which affect supply.

8.5   A fashion model can earn £800 per week modelling but her next best alternative job is as a clerical assistant earning £250 per week.

        What are her transfer earnings?

        (a)   £250

        (b)   £550

        (c)   £800

        (d)   £1,050

8.6   Opportunity cost is:

        (a)   the minimum cost at which an item can be produced.

        (b)   the loss of the next best alternative.

        (c)   the increase in variable costs due to each additional unit produced.

        (d)   also known as economic rent.

                                                        (FTC Internal Exam December 1998)

8.7   A and B each earn £250 per week as actors. In their next best employments A could earn £180 per week as a teacher and B £150 per week as a waiter. Which of the following statements about their earnings is correct?

        (a)   The economic rent accruing to both A and B is £250 per week.

        (b)   The economic rent of A is higher than that of B.

        (c)   A has transfer earnings of £70 per week.

        (d)   B derives an economic rent of £100 per week.

8.8   In which of the following situations is the demand for labour likely to be fairly elastic?

    (i)   An industry where labour costs form a small proportion of total cost.

    (ii)   An industry in which technical progress is continually developing inexpensive labour saving techniques.

    (iii)   An industry producing a good which has a very inelastic demand.

    (iv)   An industry which is labour intensive and supplies a commodity which has a very elastic demand.

    (a)   (i) and (ii).

    (b)   (ii) and (iv).

    (c)   (i), (ii) and (iv).

    (d)   (iii) only.

8.9   The supply curve of labour will be more elastic:

    (a)   the more training is required for the job.

    (b)   the greater is the immobility of labour between occupations.

    (c)   for a single firm than for the industry as a whole.

    (d)   the higher is the wage.

(May 1997)

8.10   Which one of the following will tend to make the supply of labour to a particular occupation more elastic?

    (a)   Low skill requirements.

    (b)   The need to pass professional examinations.

    (c)   High wage rates.

    (d)   A legal minimum wage.

(November 1997)

8.11   The supply of a certain factor of production is perfectly elastic. What will be the effect of a decrease in demand for the factor?

    (a)   An increase in economic rent.

    (b)   A decrease in economic rent.

    (c)   An increase in transfer earnings.

    (d)   A decrease in transfer earnings.

8.12   With a fixed supply of labour, the imposition of a minimum wage will cause most unemployment when:

   (a)   the minimum wage is below the market wage.

   (b)   the demand for labour is elastic.

   (c)   the demand for labour is inelastic.

   (d)   the demand for labour has an elasticity equal to unity.

(November 1994)

8.13   The imposition of a minimum wage will cause unemployment in a labour market only if:

   (a)   the demand for labour is elastic.

   (b)   the demand for labour is inelastic.

   (c)   the minimum wage is above the equilibrium wage.

   (d)   the minimum wage is below the equilibrium wage.

(Pilot Paper 2000)

8.14   The mobility of labour can be increased by:

   (a)   greater specialisation of labour.

   (b)   improved passenger train services.

   (c)   longer re-training periods.

   (d)   firms adopting more capital–intensive techniques.

8.15   If trade unions negotiate a wage rate above the equilibrium, which of the following will not occur?

   (a)   Part of the new supply curve of labour will be horizontal.

   (b)   Some of the existing workforce will become unemployed.

   (c)   Employers will demand more labour.

   (d)   Some workers will still only work for a wage rate above that negotiated.

8.16   Which one of the following statements is incorrect?

   (a)   Wages are determined mainly by the forces of supply and demand in imperfect markets.

   (b)   The supply of labour does not consist of homogeneous (ie uniform) units.

   (c)   An increase in wages will always result in a rise in unemployment.

   (d)   The marginal product of labour theory attempts to explain the demand for labour.

(May 1996)

8.17   The workforce of a manufacturing company are negotiating a pay rise. Which of the following arguments is most in accordance with the marginal productivity theory of wages?

(a)   Demand for the company's products has increased.

(b)   Workers require higher wages to compensate for an increase in the cost of living.

(c)   Workers in comparable trades have higher earnings.

(d)   The work has become more difficult to perform.

8.18   A rise in wages in an industry is most likely to lead to unemployment if:

(i)   the supply of substitute factors is elastic.

(ii)   labour costs are a high proportion of total costs.

(iii)   demand for the final product is price inelastic.

(iv)   supply of labour is price elastic.

Which of the above are correct?

(a)   (i) and (ii) only.

(b)   (i), (ii) and (iii) only.

(c)   (i), (ii) and (iv) only.

(d)   (iii) and (iv) only.

(May 1994)

8.19   A trade union will be least successful in raising the wages of its members in a particular firm when:

(a)   wages form a large proportion of total costs.

(b)   the demand for the product is price inelastic.

(c)   there is a low degree of substitutability between labour and capital.

(d)   demand for the product is expanding.

(May 1993)

8.20   Social capital is:

(a)   part of capital stock which includes roads and hospitals.

(b)   part of capital stock which includes private houses.

(c)   capital belonging to socialists.

(d)   capital which can easily be used by a firm.

Question 9

9.1   Which one of the following is not a potential source of market failure?

(a)   External costs.

(b)   External benefits.

(c)   An unequal income distribution.

(d)   The existence of monopolies.

(May 2001)

9.2   Externalities are:

(a)   merit goods.

(b)   public goods.

(c)   factors relating to the size and geographical concentration of an industry which tend to reduce firm's production costs.

(d)   beneficial or detrimental effects from production or consumption processes on society as a whole.

9.3   External costs (or negative externalities) imply:

(a)   an item will be produced in excessive quantity in a free market.

(b)   an industry is concentrated in one region of a country.

(c)   an item will be produced in insufficient quantity in a free market.

(d)   diseconomies of scale apply in an industry.

(FTC Internal Exam December 1998)

9.4   Which one of the following is not an example of an external social cost?

(a)   Reduction of oil reserves owing to increased use of cars.

(b)   River pollution caused by a manufacturing process.

(c)   Health problems caused by vehicle emissions.

(d)   Discarded packaging outside fast food outlets.

(Pilot Paper 2000)

9.5   A quasi public good is a good:

(a)   the consumption of which benefits society more than an individual consumer.

(b)   which markets could, in principle, provide but for some reason they do not.

(c)   which is a type of positive externality.

(d)   which is a type of demerit good.

9.6   Pure public goods are those goods:

(a)   which are produced by the government.

(b)   whose production involves no externalities.

(c)   whose consumption by one person implies less consumption by others.

(d)   where individuals cannot be excluded from consuming them.

(May 1994)

9.7   Governments may be concerned about the growth of monopoly power in an industry because monopolies:

(a)   attempt to maximise profits.

(b)   restrict output.

(c)   may secure economies of scale.

(d)   control a large share of the market.

(New Regulations Pilot 2000)

9.8   Which one of the following best describes the main purposes of the Competition Commission?

(a)   To prevent the growth of large firms.

(b)   To investigate anti-competitive behaviour by firms.

(c)   To encourage mergers to enable firms to secure economies of scale.

(d)   To regulate the prices charged by privatised utilities.

(May 1998)

9.9   Which one of the following would be a sound economic reason for the government to prevent a merger between two companies?

(a)   Combined profits would increase.

(b)   Competition would decrease and prices rise.

(c)   The industry would become more concentrated.

(d)   The companies are operating in the same industry.

(November 1998)

9.10   Which one of the following is not a valid economic reason for producing a good or service in the public sector?

(a)   The good is a basic commodity consumed by everyone.

(b)   It is a public good.

(c)   There is a natural monopoly in the production of the good.

(d)   It is a merit good.

(May 1998)

9.11   In a market economy the price system provides all of the following except which one?

(a)   An estimation of the value placed on goods by consumers.

(b)   A distribution of income according to needs.

(c)   Incentives to producers.

(d)   A means of allocating resources between different uses.

(May 1998)

9.12   Arguments for allocating resources through the market mechanism rather than through government direction include three of the following.

Which one is the exception?

(a)   It provides a more efficient means of communicating consumer wants to producers.

(b)   It ensures a fairer distribution of income.

(c)   It gives more incentive to producers to reduce costs.

(d)   It encourages companies to respond to consumer demand.

(November 1997)

9.13   Which of the following would prevent the price mechanism in a market economy from efficiently allocating resources?

(i)   External costs and benefits.
(ii)   Shortages of raw materials.
(iii)   Firms with monopoly power.
(iv)   Tariffs on imports.

(a)   (i) and (ii) only.

(b)   (ii) and (iii) only.

(c)   (i), (ii) and (iv) only.

(d)   (i) and (iii) only.

(Specimen 1994/5)

9.14   Arguments in favour of state ownership includes all of the following except which one?

(a)   Social needs, since private firms do not always take the full social costs of their decisions into account.

(b)   The need to produce essential goods.

(c)   The natural monopoly argument.

(d)   The need for effective regulation.

9.15   Imposing an indirect tax on a good will:

(a)   shift the demand curve for the good to the left.

(b)   shift the supply curve of the good to the left.

(c)   lead to market price inevitably going up by the full amount of the tax.

(d)   lead to a reduction in the market price.

9.16   An increase in an indirect tax will generate the greatest increase in revenue when the price elasticity of demand for an item is:

(a)   zero.

(b)   one.

(c)   infinity.

(d)   minus one.

(FTC Internal Exam December 1998)

9.17   Which one of the following will result if a firm is taxed by an amount equal to the external costs that its productive activities impose on society?

(a)   Resource allocation will be improved since prices more closely reflect costs and benefits.

(b)   There will be a misallocation of resources because the price mechanism has been interfered with.

(c)   The increase in costs will lead the firm to raise output in order to maintain profits.

(d)   The firm will maintain output and profits by passing the costs of the tax onto its consumers.

(November 1995)

9.18   The economic welfare case for governments increasing taxes on petrol to raise its real price is that:

(a)   oil is a scarce resource.

(b)   it would reduce the imports of oil.

(c)   there is a large demand for petrol.

(d)   petrol consumption involves external social costs.

(May 2001)

9.19   Which of the following statements about a policy of privatising a public sector industry are true?

(i)   It will permit economies of scale.
(ii)   It is a means of widening share ownership.
(iii)   The industry would become more responsive to the profit motive.
(iv)   It is a source of funds for the government.

(a)   (i) and (ii) only.

(b)   (i), (ii) and (iii) only.

(c)   (ii) and (iii) only.

(d)   (ii), (iii) and (iv) only.

(May 1997)

9.20   Which one of the following is not a valid argument for privatisation?

(a)   Taking social costs and benefits fully into account.

(b)   Encouraging an increase in productive efficiency.

(c)   Raising finance for the government.

(d)   Increasing the flexibility with which an organisation can be managed.

(FTC Internal Exam June 1999)

Question 10

10.1   In the circular flow model of the economy, the level of national income will always reach an equilibrium because:

(a)   injections and withdrawals are always equal.

(b)   withdrawals are a function of the level of income.

(c)   governments will change taxes and expenditure to ensure equilibrium.

(d)   expenditure equals income.

(May 2001)

10.2   Which of the following represents withdrawals from the circular flow of income?

(i)   Distributed profits.
(ii)   Interest paid on bank loans.
(iii)   Income tax payments.
(iv)   Imports

(a)   (i) and (ii).

(b)   (ii) and (iii) only.

(c)   (i) and (iii) only.

(d)   (iii) and (iv) only.

(May 1993)

10.3   National income is in equilibrium, with investment greater than savings. This implies that:

    (a)   imports plus taxation is greater than government spending plus exports.

    (b)   imports plus taxation is less than government spending plus exports.

    (c)   injections are greater than withdrawals.

    (d)   savings plus imports is greater than taxation plus government spending.

10.4   National income is in equilibrium when:

    (a)   demand equals supply.

    (b)   full employment is achieved.

    (c)   exports equals imports.

    (d)   injections equals withdrawals (or leakages).

(FTC Internal Exam December 1999)

10.5   The condition for national income equilibrium is:

    (a)   exports plus government expenditure plus investment equals savings plus imports plus taxation.

    (b)   leakages equal withdrawals.

    (c)   investment plus savings equals government spending plus taxation.

    (d)   aggregate demand equals aggregate supply.

(FTC Internal Exam June 1999)

10.6   Which one of the following is a transfer payment in national income accounting?

    (a)   Educational scholarships.

    (b)   Salaries of lecturers.

    (c)   Payments for textbooks.

    (d)   Payments of examination entry fees.

(November 1999)

10.7   Which one of the following would cause a fall in the level of aggregate demand in an economy?

    (a)   A decrease in the level of imports.

    (b)   A fall in the propensity to save.

    (c)   A decrease in government expenditure.

    (d)   A decrease in the level of income tax.

(May 1997)

10.8   In calculating national income, double-counting can be avoided by:

(a)   deducting taxes and adding subsidies.

(b)   deducting imports and adding exports.

(c)   excluding the value of the output of intermediate goods.

(d)   excluding the value of transactions in second hand goods.

(Pilot Paper 2000)

10.9   Gross national product will be higher than gross domestic product if:

(a)   exports of goods and services exceed imports of goods and services.

(b)   there is a net inflow of factor payments on the current account of the balance of payments.

(c)   there is a net inflow on the capital account of the balance of payments.

(d)   government taxation exceeds government expenditure.

(May 2001)

10.10   GNP (Gross National Product) at factor cost may be best defined as:

(a)   the total of goods and services produced within an economy over a given period of time.

(b)   the total expenditure of consumers on domestically produced goods and services.

(c)   all incomes received by residents in a country in return for factor services provided domestically or abroad.

(d)   the value of total output produced domestically plus net interest, profit and dividends from abroad minus capital consumption.

(Specimen 1994/95)

10.11   Gross value added at basic cost is equal to:

(a)   gross national product at factor cost.

(b)   gross national product at market prices.

(c)   gross domestic product at factor cost.

(d)   gross domestic product at market prices.

10.12   Gross domestic product at market price equals:

(a)   national income plus capital consumption less net interest, profit and dividends from abroad, plus taxes on expenditure minus subsidies.

(b)   national income less capital consumption less net interest, profit and dividends from abroad, plus subsidies less taxes on expenditure.

(c)   gross domestic product at factor cost less taxes plus subsidies.

(d)   gross national product plus exports less imports.

10.13   Which of the following will cause a decrease in the multiplier?

(a)   A fall in the marginal propensity to import.

(b)   A rise in the marginal propensity to consume.

(c)   A rise in the marginal social tax rate.

(d)   A fall in the marginal propensity to save.

10.14   Gross national product equals:

(a)   national income plus net investment income from abroad.

(b)   net national product plus capital consumption.

(c)   gross domestic product plus exports minus imports.

(d)   gross domestic product plus taxes on expenditure minus subsidies.

10.15   Net national product equals:

(a)   gross domestic product plus capital consumption.

(b)   gross national product plus exports minus imports.

(c)   gross national product minus capital consumption.

(d)   gross domestic product plus net investment income from abroad.

(FTC Internal Exam June 1998)

10.16   The elements of aggregate demand are:

(a) $C + I + G + X + M$

(b) $C + I + G + X - M$

(c) $C + I - G + X - M$

(d) $C + I - G - X + M$

10.17   In an economy where out of every £100 of national income, £25 is paid in tax, £10 is spent on imports and £15 is saved, the value of the multiplier will be:

(a)   2

(b)   2.5

(c)   5

(d)   10

(November 1993)

10.18   The marginal propensity to consume is best defined as:

(a)   the proportion of additional income that is spent on consumer goods.

(b)   the proportion of additional income that is spent on imported goods.

(c)   the amount of utility derived from the consumption of an extra unit of a good or service.

(d)   the proportion of consumer incomes that is spent on consumer durable goods.

(November 1994)

10.19   The marginal social tax rate is 0.2; the marginal propensity to import is 0.1; the marginal propensity to save is 0.1. What is the value of the multiplier?

(a)   2.5

(b)   1.67

(c)   0.6

(d)   5

10.20   Given a marginal propensity to consume of 0.60, an increase in exports of £2 billion will cause national income:

(a)   to rise by £3.5 billion.

(b)   to fall by £5.0 billion.

(c)   to fall by £3.5 billion.

(d)   to rise by £5.0 billion.

(FTC Internal Exam June 1998)

Question 11

11.1   Which of the following is characteristic of a boom in a trade cycle?

(a)   Heavy unemployment.

(b)   Surplus stocks.

(c)   Firms begin to invest.

(d)   High levels of investment.

11.2   Which one of the following is not a normal feature of the upswing phase of the trade cycle?

(a)   Falling unemployment.

(b)   Rising levels of imports.

(c)   Rising national income.

(d)   Increasing government borrowing.

(Pilot Paper 2000)

11.3   Which of the following is most likely to lead to an increase in consumption?

(a)   A decrease in interest rates.

(b)   Falling property values.

(c)   Increases in taxation.

(d)   Credit less available.

11.4   'Keynesian' unemployment is an alternative term for which of the following types of unemployment?

(a)   Frictional.

(b)   Seasonal.

(c)   Structural.

(d)   Cyclical.

11.5   Structural unemployment is best defined as that caused by:

(a)   the long term decline of particular industries.

(b)   the trade cycle.

(c)   an insufficient level of aggregate demand.

(d)   seasonal variations in demand for particular goods and services.

(May 1996)

11.6   Structural unemployment is caused by:

(a)   long-term decline in demand for an industry's products.

(b)   falling levels of aggregate demand.

(c)   high levels of inflation.

(d)   a downturn in national economic activity.

(Pilot Paper 2000)

11.7   Unemployment caused by technological change may be regarded as:

(a)   structural.

(b)   frictional.

(c)   temporary.

(d)   residual.

11.8   The Labour Force Survey:

(a)   is a survey of people in work.

(b)   is a survey estimating the number of people out of work and seeking employment.

(c)   measures people registered as unemployed and claiming benefits.

(d)   measures the number of people in work.

11.9   Cyclical unemployment refers to unemployment:

(a)   which occurs because of the seasonal nature of some industries.

(b)   resulting from the long-term decline of an industry.

(c)   which occurs at particular times of the year.

(d)   which occurs during recessions.

(May 2001)

11.10   Cyclical unemployment:

(a)   is caused by seasonal changes in the demand for labour.

(b)   is caused by rapid technological change.

(c)   is the result of inadequate supply side policies.

(d)   is caused by a lack of effective demand during a recession.

(FTC Internal Exam December 1999)

11.11   The Quantity Theory of Money will not be valid if:

(a)   the velocity of circulation should depend inversely on the money supply.

(b)   real output should be independent of the money supply.

(c)   it is possible to define and measure the money supply.

(d)   the price level depends on the money supply.

11.12   A country is experiencing a high rate of inflation which is expected to continue for several years. Other things being equal, which of the following is most likely to lose out as a result of the inflation?

(a)   An art collector.

(b)   An investor holding shares in a blue chip company.

(c)   A lender.

(d)   A borrower.

11.13 Which of the following is the basic concept which underlies the accelerator theory of investment?

(a)   Investment depends on the level of savings.

(b)   Investment is inversely related to the rate of interest.

(c)   Investment is determined by the level of commercial bank lending.

(d)   Investment rises when there is an increase in the rate of growth of demand in the economy.

(May 1994)

11.14 The accelerator is:

(a)   the amount by which national income rises in response to a given increase in investment.

(b)   the amount by which investment rises following a given increase in demand.

(c)   the amount of net investment necessary to increase output by one unit.

(d)   the amount by which commercial banks can independently increase the money supply given an increase in their cash reserves of £1.

11.15 All of the following are disadvantages of inflation except which one?

(a)   It redistributes wealth from debtors to creditors.

(b)   It reduces international competitiveness.

(c)   Market price signals are distorted.

(d)   Fixed income earners experience a fall in real income.

(May 2001)

11.16 Assuming that the economy is operating at full employment, which of the following would be most likely to lead to inflation?

(a)   A fall in the level of private investment.

(b)   A rise in the productivity of labour.

(c)   A rise in the volume of imports.

(d)   A reduction in direct taxation.

(November 1993)

11.17 The government budget deficit is best defined as:

(a)   the total borrowing by the general public over the period of a year.

(b)   the amount of borrowing needed to finance the difference between a country's exports and its imports.

(c)   the amount of taxation and borrowing needed to finance public expenditure.

(d)   the difference between government expenditure and its revenue from taxation.

(November 1994)

11.18   Which one of the following would appear as a debit item in the balance of payments?

(a)   Payment of interest on debts owed to overseas commercial banks.

(b)   Expenditure by tourists visiting the country.

(c)   Overseas capital investment by domestic companies.

(d)   Repayment of debts to overseas central banks.

(May 1996)

11.19   Which of the following are included as invisible items on the current account of the balance of payments?

(i)   Inflows of capital investment.
(ii)   Flows of profits from assets held overseas.
(iii)   Expenditure by foreign tourists within the country.
(iv)   Interest payments received from bank accounts held in other countries.

(a)   (i), (ii) and (iii) only.

(b)   (i), (ii) and (iv) only.

(c)   (i), (iii) and (iv) only.

(d)   (ii), (iii) and (iv) only.

(May 1994)

11.20   Which of the following will be included in the capital account of the balance of payments?

(a)   Export of a manufactured good.

(b)   Expenditure by a citizen on a foreign holiday.

(c)   Interest received on an overseas investment.

(d)   Transfers of capital by government.

Question 12

12.1   Which of the following is inconsistent with a deflationary (tight) fiscal policy?

(a)   Decreased government borrowing.

(b)   Higher direct taxation.

(c)   Higher government expenditure.

(d)   Higher indirect taxation.

(FTC Internal Exam December 1999)

12.2   An expansionary fiscal policy would be most likely to reduce unemployment if the country had:

(a)   a high marginal propensity to import.

(b)   a low marginal propensity to save.

(c)   a high marginal tax rate.

(d)   a low marginal propensity to consume.

(May 2001)

12.3   The effect on a business of a contractionary fiscal policy will be greatest when the business:

(a)   has a high gearing ratio.

(b)   produces a good with a high income elasticity of demand.

(c)   produces non-durable goods.

(d)   exports a high proportion of its output.

(May 2001)

12.4   Which of the following would, other things being equal, contribute to reduction of inflationary pressure in an economy?

(i)   A fall in the volume of exports.
(ii)   A rise in the volume of imports.
(iii)   A decrease in the level of direct taxation.
(iv)   An increase in the level of public expenditure.

(a)   (i) and (ii) only.

(b)   (ii), (iii) and (iv) only.

(c)   (iii) and (iv) only.

(d)   (iii) only.

(Specimen 1994/95)

12.5   Monetarists believe that inflation will follow from:

(a)   excessive demand for money in the economy.

(b)   trade unions demanding higher wage rates.

(c)   expansion of the money supply.

(d)   firms and individuals spending their excess money balances.

(May 2001)

12.6   Governments wish to control inflation because it:

(a)   tends to reduce government tax revenue.

(b)   causes the money supply to expand.

(c)   damages international competitiveness.

(d)   shifts income towards holders of financial assets.

(Pilot Paper 2000)

12.7   According to advocates of supply side economics, which of the following measures is most likely to reduce unemployment in an economy?

(a)   Increasing labour re-training schemes.

(b)   Increasing public sector investment.

(c)   Increasing the level of benefits paid to the unemployed.

(d)   Decreasing the money supply.

(May 1993)

12.8   Which one of the following would be part of a supply side policy to reduce unemployment in an economy?

(a)   Reducing the supply of imports by raising trade barriers.

(b)   Increasing labour re-training schemes.

(c)   Public expenditure to increase the supply of merit goods.

(d)   Supplying government subsidies to declining industries.

(Pilot Paper 2000)

12.9   The real rate of interest is defined as the:

(a)   rate of interest banks actually charge their customers.

(b)   annualised percentage rate of interest.

(c)   yield on undated fixed interest government securities.

(d)   difference between the money rate of interest and the inflation rate.

(May 2001)

12.10   The crowding out effect occurs when a:

(a)   rise in interest rates reduces private investment.

(b)   rise in interest rates reduces the demand for money.

(c)   fall in interest rates discourages saving.

(d)   rise in interest rates raises mortgage rates.

(May 2001)

12.11   A rise in interest rates in a country can be expected to lead to all of the following except which one?

(a)   A fall in share prices.

(b)   A rise in investment.

(c)   A rise in the exchange rate.

(d)   A shift of income from borrowers to savers.

(Pilot Paper 2000)

12.12   Which one of the following is likely to result from an increase in the size of the public sector borrowing requirement?

(a)   A decrease in the rate of inflation.

(b)   A reduction in the level of taxation.

(c)   A rise in the price of shares.

(d)   A rise in the rate of interest.

(November 1997)

12.13   Which one of the following can be used by governments to finance a budget deficit?

(a)   A rise in direct taxation.

(b)   The sale of public assets.

(c)   An increase in interest rates.

(d)   An issue of government savings certificates.

(Specimen 1994/95)

12.14   Inequality in the distribution of income in an economy is most likely to decrease when:

(a)   indirect taxation is constant and direct taxation rises.

(b)   indirect taxation falls and direct taxation rises.

(c)   indirect taxation rises and direct taxation falls.

(d)   indirect taxation is constant and direct taxation falls.

(November 1993)

12.15   A regressive tax is:

(a)   socially inequitable.

(b)   one that takes more from the poor than from the rich.

(c)   one that takes more from those on lower incomes than from those on higher incomes.

(d)   one that takes a higher proportion of the incomes of those on lower incomes.

12.16   A progressive system of taxation is:

    (a)   one that is fair.

    (b)   one that takes a higher proportion of the incomes of individuals with higher taxable incomes.

    (c)   one that takes more money from the rich than from the poor.

    (d)   one where as your income increases by x%, your tax liability also increases by x%.

12.17   Which of the following are likely consequences of a fall in interest rates?

    (i)   A rise in the demand for consumer credit.
    (ii)   A fall in investment.
    (iii)   A fall in government expenditure.
    (iv)   A rise in the demand for housing.

    (a)   (i) and (ii) only.

    (b)   (i), (ii) and (iii) only.

    (c)   (i), (iii) and (iv) only.

    (d)   (ii), (iii) and (iv) only.

(Specimen 1994/95)

12.18   In the theory of the demand for money, the transactions demand for money is determined by the:

    (a)   level of consumers' incomes.

    (b)   expected changes in interest rates.

    (c)   expected changes in bond prices.

    (d)   level of notes and coins in circulation.

(May 1997)

12.19   All of the following measures might be used to help reduce demand pull inflation except:

    (a)   an increase in the basic rate of income tax.

    (b)   a decrease in interest rates.

    (c)   a decrease in government expenditure.

    (d)   an increase in the higher marginal tax rate.

(FTC Internal Exam December 1998)

12.20   If a government wished to reduce the rate of inflation, which of the following policies would be appropriate?

(i)   A rise in the level of taxation.
(ii)   A reduction in the level of public expenditure.
(iii)   Restrictions in the level of imports.
(iv)   Reductions in the growth of the money supply.

(a)   (i), (ii) and (iii) only.

(b)   (ii), (iii) and (iv) only.

(c)   (ii) and (iv) only.

(d)   (i), (ii) and (iv) only.

(November 1994)

Question 13

13.1   What does the phrase 'one of the functions of money is as a standard of deferred payment' mean?

(a)   Money is an alternative to barter.

(b)   Money is a liquid asset used for exchange purposes.

(c)   Money is a measure of value.

(d)   Money must maintain its value over time.

13.2   Which of the following is not a function of money?

(a)   Portability.

(b)   Medium of exchange.

(c)   Store of value.

(d)   Unit of account.

13.3   Which of the following are functions of money?

(i)   A medium of exchange.
(ii)   A store of value.
(iii)   A unit of account.
(iv)   A measure of liquidity.

(a)   (i) and (ii) only.

(b)   (i), (ii) and (iii) only.

(c)   (ii), (iii) and (iv) only.

(d)   All of them.

(November 1999)

13.4   Which is the best description of the broad supply of money in an economy?

(a)   Notes and coins issued by the central bank.

(b)   Money created by the commercial banks.

(c)   Coins, notes and bank deposits.

(d)   All items of legal tender.

(May 1993)

13.5   Which of the following is not included in the money supply measure known as M0?

(a)   Notes and coins in circulation.

(b)   Banks' and building societies' till money.

(c)   Foreign currency deposits of UK residents with UK banks and building societies.

(d)   Banks' operational balances with the Bank of England.

13.6   Which of the following would lead to a rise in the demand for money?

(i)   A rise in disposable incomes.
(ii)   A fall in interest rates.
(iii)   An expectation of falling share prices.
(iv)   A decrease in the money supply.

(a)   (i) and (ii) only.

(b)   (ii) and (iii) only.

(c)   (ii), (iii) and (iv) only.

(d)   (i), (ii) and (iii) only.

(May 1998)

13.7   Which of the following is not consistent with a deflationary monetary policy?

(a)   Central bank purchases of bills on the open market.

(b)   Calling for special deposits.

(c)   Overfunding a fiscal deficit.

(d)   An increase in bank base rates.

13.8   Which of the following is most likely to lead to a fall in the money supply?

(a)   A fall in interest rates.

(b)   Purchases of government securities by the central bank.

(c)   Sales of government securities by the central bank.

(d)   A rise in the amount of cash held by commercial banks.

(November 1993)

13.9   If all the banks in an economy operate on a cash reserve ratio of 20%, how much cash would have to be deposited in banks for the money supply to increase by £50 million?

   (a)   £8 million

   (b)   £12.5 million

   (c)   £10 million

   (d)   £5 million

13.10   A country's money supply increased by 25%. The velocity of circulation fell by 5%. Prices increased, on average, by 11%. What happened to real output?

   (a)   It increased by about 9%.

   (b)   It increased by about 6%.

   (c)   It increased by about 22%.

   (d)   It fell by about 9%.

13.11   Which of the following is not a function of commercial financial intermediaries?

   (a)   Providing maturity transformation.

   (b)   Issuing gilts.

   (c)   Aggregation.

   (d)   Reducing transaction costs.

13.12   Which of the following is an investment institution?

   (a)   Commercial bank.

   (b)   Insurance company.

   (c)   Building society.

   (d)   Credit card company.

13.13   Which one of the following does not form part of the equity capital market?

   (a)   Life assurance companies.

   (b)   Pension funds.

   (c)   Retail banks.

   (d)   Venture capitalists.

(May 2001)

13.14   Which one of the following is the most profitable to a commercial bank?

(a)   Advances to customers.

(b)   Balances with the central bank.

(c)   Money at call.

(d)   Treasury bills.

(November 1999)

13.15   Many building societies are now performing functions which are increasingly similar to commercial banks because they:

(a)   pay interest on all their deposit accounts.

(b)   have more branches than many banks.

(c)   provide full cheque accounts and money transfer services.

(d)   have a significantly greater level of deposits than banks.

(November 1999)

13.16   Which one of the following would appear as a liability in a clearing bank's balance sheet?

(a)   Advances to customers.

(b)   Money at call and short notice.

(c)   Customers' deposit accounts.

(d)   Discounted bills.

(May 1998)

13.17   Which of the following are functions which can be performed by central banks?

(i)   Issuing notes and coins.
(ii)   Supervision of banking systems.
(iii)   Conducting fiscal policy on behalf of governments.
(iv)   Holding foreign exchange reserves.

(a)   (i), (ii) and (iii) only.

(b)   (i), (ii) and (iv) only.

(c)   (i), (iii) and (iv) only.

(d)   (ii), (iii) and (iv) only.

(May 1997)

13.18   Which one of the following is not an asset of a commercial bank?

(a)   Balances at the central bank.

(b)   Money at call.

(c)   Customers' deposits.

(d)   Advances to customers.

(May 1995)

13.19 Which of the following does not engage in the buying and selling of shares for other companies?

   (a)   Investment trusts.

   (b)   Stock exchanges.

   (c)   Insurance companies.

   (d)   Pension funds.

(Specimen 1994/95)

13.20 Which of the following is not one of the benefits of financial intermediation?

   (a)   A rising stock market.

   (b)   Maturity transformation.

   (c)   Risk spreading.

   (d)   Increased convenience for borrowers and savers.

(FTC Internal Exam June 1999)

Question 14

14.1 A currency may depreciate due to:

   (a)   falling domestic interest rates.

   (b)   falling foreign currency interest rates.

   (c)   an increase in exports of goods and services.

   (d)   an expectation of falling inflation.

(FTC Internal Exam June 1998)

14.2 Which one of the following is a characteristic of floating (flexible) exchange rates?

   (a)   They provide automatic correction for balance of payments deficits and surpluses.

   (b)   They reduce uncertainty for businesses.

   (c)   Transactions costs involved in exchanging currencies are eliminated.

   (d)   They limit the ability of governments to adopt expansionary policies.

(November 1996)

14.3 Which of the following best defines the terms of trade?

   (a)   The difference between the volume of exports and imports.

   (b)   The difference between the value of imports and exports.

   (c)   The rate at which imports and exports exchange for each other.

   (d)   The rate at which currencies exchange for each other.

(November 1993)

14.4 Which of the following policies for correcting a balance of payments deficit is an expenditure reducing policy?

(a)   Cutting the level of public expenditure.

(b)   Devaluation of the currency.

(c)   The imposition of an import tax.

(d)   The use of import quotas.

(May 1997)

14.5 Which of the following might cause a country's exports to decrease?

(a)   A fall in the exchange rate for that country's currency.

(b)   A reduction in other countries' tariff barriers.

(c)   A decrease in the marginal propensity to import in other countries.

(d)   A rise in that country's imports.

(May 1995)

14.6 A rise in interest rates in an economy can be expected to lead to all of the following except which one?

(a)   A fall in share prices.

(b)   A rise in investment.

(c)   A rise in the exchange rate.

(d)   A shift of income from borrowers to savers.

(New Regulations Pilot 2000)

14.7 A devaluation of the exchange rate for a country's currency will normally result in:

(i)   a reduction in the current account deficit.
(ii)   an improvement in the country's terms of trade.
(iii)   a reduction in the domestic cost of living.
(iv)   an increased level of domestic economic activity.

(a)   (i) and (ii) only.

(b)   (i) and (iv) only.

(c)   (ii) and (iii) only.

(d)   (ii) and (iv) only.

(Specimen 1994/95)

14.8 If the exchange rate for a country's currency fell, the result would be that export prices:

(a)   measured in the domestic currency would fall.

(b)   measured in the domestic currency would rise.

(c)   measured in foreign currency would fall.

(d)   measured in foreign currency would rise.

(Pilot Paper 2000)

14.9   Which of the following are the functions of the World Trade Organisation (WTO)?

   (i)   Encouraging reductions in tariff levels.
   (ii)   Discouraging the growth of non-tariff barriers to trade.
   (iii)   Encouraging the formation of customs unions and free trade areas.
   (iv)   Providing funds for countries with balance of payments difficulties.

   (a)   (i) and (ii) only.

   (b)   (ii) and (iii) only.

   (c)   (i), (ii) and (iv) only.

   (d)   (i), (iii) and (iv) only.

(November 1994)

14.10   Intra-industry trade occurs when a country:

   (a)   imports and exports the products of the same industry.

   (b)   imports and exports the products of different industries.

   (c)   imports goods needed as inputs to its domestic industries.

   (d)   imports goods which are also produced domestically.

(Pilot Paper 2000)

14.11   Which one of the following is not associated with the process of the globalisation of production?

   (a)   Rising trade ratios for economies.

   (b)   Concentration of production close to markets.

   (c)   Increasing production by transnational corporations.

   (d)   Increased international factor mobility.

(Pilot Paper 2000)

14.12   All of the following are characteristics of the process of globalisation except which one?

   (a)   Increased international specialisation.

   (b)   Greater integration of production in manufacturing.

   (c)   Higher levels of international trade.

   (d)   Movement of manufacturing industries to low labour cost locations.

(May 2001)

14.13   Which of the following would increase the potential benefits from international trade?

(i)   The existence of economies of scale in production.
(ii)   A high mobility of capital and labour between economies.
(iii)   Large differences in the opportunity costs of production between countries.
(iv)   Low international transport costs.

(a)   (i), (ii) and (iii) only.

(b)   (ii), (iii) and (iv) only.

(c)   (i), (iii) and (iv) only.

(d)   All of them.

(November 1999)

14.14   The theory of comparative advantage suggests that countries should:

(a)   diversify their production as much as possible.

(b)   engage in trade if the opportunity costs of production differ between countries.

(c)   engage in trade only if each country has an absolute advantage in at least one good or service.

(d)   aim to make their economies sell sufficient.

(November 1997)

14.15   If a country can produce all goods more efficiently than its trading partner, it should export:

(a)   no goods.

(b)   only those goods in which it has an absolute advantage.

(c)   only those goods in which its efficiency advantage is greatest.

(d)   all goods.

(May 2001)

14.16   An increase in the international mobility of factors of production leads to:

(a)   an increase in international trade.

(b)   increased unemployment in low wage economies.

(c)   increasing differences in wage rates between countries.

(d)   decreasing differences in factor prices between countries.

(May 2001)

14.17   All of the following are reasons for transnational companies locating production of a good in more than one country except one. Which one is the exception?

   (a)   The existence of trade barriers.

   (b)   Significant transport costs.

   (c)   Economies of scale in production.

   (d)   Differences in demand conditions between countries.

(May 2001)

14.18   Which one of the following is not a benefit of adopting a single currency within a trading bloc of countries?

   (a)   A reduction in international transactions costs.

   (b)   The elimination of exchange rate uncertainty.

   (c)   The ability for each country to adopt an independent monetary policy.

   (d)   Increased international price transparency.

(Pilot Paper 2000)

14.19   Which one of the following would be likely to result in a rise in the value of UK sterling against the Euro?

   (a)   A rise in interest rates in the UK.

   (b)   The UK central bank buying Euros in exchange for sterling.

   (c)   A rise in interest rates in the Euro zone.

   (d)   Increased capital flows from the UK to the Euro zone.

(May 2001)

14.20   All of the following are characteristics of a common market except which one?

   (a)   Free trade in goods and services among member states.

   (b)   Common levels of direct taxation.

   (c)   Free movement of factors of production between member states.

   (d)   A common external tariff.

(May 2001)

Question 15

15.1   Michael Dawson receives a cloth cap factory, complete with machinery, due to a bequest (this example assumes no taxation on bequests). He could lease it out at a market rent of £12,000 per year, but chooses instead to put it to use. He withdraws £100,000 of his own money, which had previously earned 15% interest per year, from his bank and invests it in the business. He gives up his old job as a civil servant, from which he had earned £14,000 salary per year, to run the business.

   In its first year, Michael Dawson's accountants estimate his business to have incurred £114,000 of expenses, including a salary of £8,000 paid to Mr Dawson.

   What level of opportunity costs did this business incur?

   (a)   £115,000

   (b)   £33,000

   (c)   £147,000

   (d)   £122,000

15.2   Which one of the following would shift a country's production possibility frontier (PPF) outwards (to the right)?

   (a)   A fall in unemployment.

   (b)   An increase in exports.

   (c)   A rise in total consumer expenditure.

   (d)   Technical progress reducing production costs.

   (New Regulations Pilot 2000)

15.3   Which one of the following is a feature of a market economy?

   (a)   Prices are determined mainly by market forces.

   (b)   Resources are allocated between different markets by administrative decisions.

   (c)   Consumer preferences are determined by market research.

   (d)   All markets are characterised by a high degree of competition.

   (New Regulations Pilot 2000)

15.4   Which one of the following is not a factor of production?

   (a)   Unskilled labour.

   (b)   A machine tool.

   (c)   Cash reserves.

   (d)   Entrepreneurship.

   (New Regulations Pilot 2000)

15.5   When a government wishes to increase its expenditure on education, but can do so only at the expense of expenditure elsewhere, this is said to be an example of:

(a)   diminishing marginal utility.

(b)   opportunity costs.

(c)   scale of preferences.

(d)   equi-marginal returns.

(May 1995)

15.6   The 'central economic problem' refers to:

(a)   the persistence of unemployment.

(b)   the need to allocate scarce resources between competing uses.

(c)   consumers having less money than they would like.

(d)   the need to ensure that in the long run all production costs are covered by sales revenue.

(New Regulations Pilot 2000)

15.7   Economics is concerned with:

(a)   government policies.

(b)   money.

(c)   the allocation of scarce resources.

(d)   unemployment and inflation.

(FTC Internal Exam June 1999)

15.8   Which of the following is not a feature of monopolistic competition?

(a)   A large number of firms in the industry.

(b)   A homogeneous product.

(c)   No barriers to the entry or exit of firms.

(d)   Product differentiation.

(May 1993)

15.9   The demand curve for the product of a business will shift to the right when there is:

(a)   a reduction in indirect tax on the good.

(b)   an improvement in production which lowers costs.

(c)   a fall in the price of the good.

(d)   an increase in the supply of a complementary good.

(New Regulations Pilot 2000)

15.10   The existence of international trade is best explained by the fact that countries:

    (a)   use different currencies.

    (b)   have different economic systems.

    (c)   have different endowments of factors of production.

    (d)   have specialised in different goods and services.

(May 1994)

15.11   The term 'mixed economy' implies all of the following conditions except which one?

    (a)   The allocation of resources is mainly through the price system.

    (b)   Producers have an incentive to advertise their products.

    (c)   There is some government planning of the use of resources.

    (d)   All industries have a mix of small and large companies.

(May 1996)

15.12   Venture capital is best described as:

    (a)   investment funds provided for established companies.

    (b)   short-term investment in Eurocurrency markets.

    (c)   capital funds that are highly mobile between financial centres.

    (d)   equity finance in high risk enterprises.

(May 1997)

15.13   Other things being equal, all of the following would lead to a rise in share prices except which one?

    (a)   A rise in interest rates.

    (b)   A reduction in corporation tax.

    (c)   A rise in company profits.

    (d)   A decline in the number of new share issues.

(May 1998)

15.14   Which one of the following statements about profit is correct?

    (a)   In the private sector, the profit motive encourages efficiency.

    (b)   Nationalised industries are always inefficient because they are not profit motivated.

    (c)   Not-for-profit organisations do not have to worry about being efficient.

    (d)   In the private sector, companies cannot be profitable unless they are efficient.

(November 1998)

15.15   The short run average cost curve for firms rises after a certain level of output because of:

   (a)   diseconomies of scale.

   (b)   the law of diminishing returns.

   (c)   diminishing marginal utility.

   (d)   rising price of factors of production.

   (New Regulations Pilot 2000)

15.16   A policy of fiscal expansion is most likely to reduce unemployment when:

   (a)   there is a high marginal propensity to consume.

   (b)   there is a high marginal propensity to save.

   (c)   unemployment is mainly of a structural kind.

   (d)   there is a fixed exchange rate.

   (May 1994)

15.17   Which of the following does not represent a market failure in a free market system?

   (a)   A lack of incentives.

   (b)   Monopoly power.

   (c)   Negative externalities.

   (d)   Positive externalities.

   (FTC Internal Exam December 1999)

15.18   If the demand curve for a good is price inelastic, then the effect of a rise in the price of the good will be that:

   (a)   the quantity sold and total consumer expenditure on the good will both rise.

   (b)   the quantity sold will fall, but the total consumer expenditure on the good will rise.

   (c)   the quantity sold will rise, but the total consumer expenditure on the good will fall.

   (d)   the quantity sold and total consumer expenditure on the good will both fall.

   (November 1993)

15.19   In economics, 'the central economic problem' means:

   (a)   consumers do not have as much money as they would wish.

   (b)   there will always be a certain level of unemployment.

   (c)   resources are not always allocated in an optimal way.

   (d)   output is restricted by the limited availability of resources.

   (May 1993)

15.20   Opportunity costs are:

(a)   the increase in costs due to the last unit of output produced.

(b)   the next best alternative which has been foregone.

(c)   variable (rather than fixed) costs.

(d)   less than accounting costs, in a profit maximising business.

(FTC Internal Exam June 1999)

Objective Test Answers

Answer 1

(a)   (i)   .... the value of the next best alternative output.

       (ii)   .... from A to either B or C (*any combination of moves between A, B and C*).

(b)   .... to be **foregone** to acquire more **consumer** goods.

(c)   (i)   D.   Inside the PPF, output less than maximum with full employment of resources.

       (ii)   Outward movement of PPF from PPF1 to PPF2.

(d)   (i)   Employ more factors of production to produce output.

       (ii)   Raise the productivity of factors of production.

(e)   (i)   Relationship between inputs of resources and output.

       (ii)   Any three of technological progress, investments in human capital through increased labour education and training, economies of scale, improved organisation of production and its management, shifts in resources from low productivity sectors to high productivity sectors, movement of labour from low productivity to high productivity occupations.

Answer 2

(a)

Quantity sold	Total revenue £	Marginal revenue £	Average cost £
1	16	16	20
2	28	12	12.5
3	36	8	10
4	40	4	8.5
5	40	0	9
6	36	-4	11
7	28	-8	15.71

(b)   (i)   .... a measure of the responsiveness of demand to a change in price.

       (ii) $-\frac{1}{4} \div +\frac{2}{10} = -\frac{1}{4} \times 5$

              $= -\frac{5}{4}$

              $= -1.25$

(c)   (i)   Profits are maximised at the output level where **marginal cost** equals **marginal revenue**.

        (ii)   4 units.

        (iii)   £40 – 34 = £6

(d)   (i)   U shaped

        (ii)   ….. the output generated by each additional unit of input will eventually fall.

Answer 3

(a)   (i)   Consumer expenditure, investment expenditure, government expenditure and net exports.

        (ii)   (Where income and expenditure are equal). Point C at income level D.

        (iii)   (Level of expenditure less than level of income). Gap EF.

(b)

		Effect on the components of expenditure	*Impact on the equilibrium level of national income*
(i)	An increase in the marginal propensity to save	Savings up Consumption down	Fall
(ii)	A move towards surplus on the current account of the balance of payments	Net exports up	Rise
(iii)	A decrease in taxation	Consumption up	Rise
(iv)	An increase in stockholding by businesses	Investment up	Rise

(c)

If the government used interest rate policy to raise the equilibrium level of national income, they would reduce interest rates	*True or False*
A reduction in interest rates will reduce consumption	*True or False*
A reduction in interest rates will increase investment	*True or False*

(d)   Either:

        Sales and revenue may change; or

        Change in costs due to change in costs of borrowing, especially if gearing ratio is high.

Answer 4

(a)   (i)   Trade in goods, trade in services, investment income and current transfers.

          (ii)   Current transfers and transfers of capital by government.

          (iii)   Short and long term investments.

(b)   (i) $(164 - 184) = £20$ bn deficit.

          (ii) $(164 + 62 + 114 + 15) - (184 + 50 + 98 + 21) = £2$ bn surplus

          (iii) $+2 + (1 - 0.7) + (108 - 117) = £6.7$bn credit.

(c)   (i)   Real investment is investment in assets such as factories.

          (ii)   Portfolio investment is investment in stocks and shares etc.

(d)

The foreign exchange price of exports will rise	**True** or False
The domestic price of imports will fall	**True** or False
If the demand for imports and exports is price elastic, the current account will move towards deficit	**True** or False

(e)

An appreciation in a country's currency will affect the costs of a business in that country. The costs of imported components or raw materials will **fall**. This will tend to **reduce** output prices. However, the demand for the business's output may **fall** because imports become **cheaper**.

Answer 5

Note: *Answers are shown in standard text: the stems of questions requiring completion (ie missing words) are shown in bold.*

(a)   (i)   For a single firm, economies of scale are those factors which lead to **a reduction in average costs as the scale of output is increased**.

          (ii)   For a single firm, the short run average cost curve is U shaped because of the law of **diminishing returns to a fixed factor**.

(b)   Any three from

        ♦   Technical economies of scale

        ♦   Commercial economies of scale

        ♦   Managerial economies of scale

        ♦   Risk bearing economies of scale

        ♦   Financial economies of scale

(c)   (i)   Constant returns to scale.

       (ii)   Output level C

       (iii) Scale/size of factory 2.

       (iv)   2 factories of scale 5, each producing 600 units.

(d)   External economies of scale lead to a reduction in the **costs** of **firms** when the size of the **industry** increases.

(e)   (i)   All the cost curves would shift downwards.

       (ii)   The point B, where constant returns to scale start, would shift to the left.

Answer 6

(a)   (i)   Years 4 and 5.

       (ii)   Year 1: 0.7%

              Year 2: 1.0% (simple subtraction calculation)

(b)   (i)   The relationship is inverse, when unemployment falls (rises), inflation rises (falls).

       (ii)   The relationship between inflation and unemployment in years 9 and 10 can be explained by a shift to the **right** in the aggregate **supply** curve.

(c)   (i)   Cost push

       (ii)   Demand pull

       (iii) Cost push

       (iv)   Demand pull *(This is the CIMA answer, but it could be argued that increased wages will increase input costs, so causing cost push inflation.)*

(d)   (i)   False

       (ii)   True

       (iii) False

       (iv)   True

Answer 7

(a)   (i)   ...... level of output at which most economies of scale have been secured (or .... point at which the long run average cost curve levels out).

       (ii)   ..... working together with the intention of achieving the lowest possible cost of production.

(b)   (i)   The long run average cost curve for the industry.

       (ii)   Around 8m units (5m – 9m acceptable).

(iii) (a) Fiat (ie below the LRAC)

(b) Toyota (ie above the LRAC)

(iv) The most x-efficient firms are the ones in the diagram which are **below** the dotted line. This is because they have **lower** than average, average **costs** for the industry.

(c) (i) Technical, financial, managerial.

(ii) Any two from: capital, indivisibilities, bulk buying, R&D, marketing, advertising.

Answer 8

(a) (i) D (ii) OA (iii) FDIJ

(b) (i) It will rise

(ii) It will fall.

(iii) Fall

(c)

	Effect on AR &MR curves	Effect on equilibrium price and output
(i) Consumer incomes rise	Shift to right	Both rise
(ii) New firms enter the industry	Shift to left	Both fall

(d) (i) They are the mechanisms by which potential competitors are blocked.

(ii) Any four from: patents and trademarks, control over supplies, cost advantages, legislation, high start up costs, control over outlets, product differentiation etc.

Answer 9

(a) (i) D (ii) C (iii) H (iv) J (v) G

(b) (i) Investment, exports, government expenditure.

(ii) Savings, imports, taxation.

(c) (i) The level of household consumption will fall so the demand for the business sector's output will fall; or

Increased savings may lead to a fall in the interest rate so lowering costs for businesses.

(ii) This will make exports relatively more expensive so businesses will export less; or

Import prices fall so businesses lose sales to imported goods but cheaper imports will reduce costs.

(d) …….. the proportion of a small increase in income that is spent rather than saved.

Answer 10

(a)   Westland

(b)

	Westland	*Eastland*
Coffee	½ wheat	3 wheat
Wheat	2 coffee	⅓ coffee

(c)   (i)   280 tons

        (ii)   120 tons ($^{80}\!/_1 \times 1.5$)

(d)   (i)   The ratio of the index of average export prices divided by the index of average import prices.

        (ii)   There will be a change in the terms of trade if there is a change in the **exchange** rate. A depreciation leads to **falling** export prices and **rising** import prices. This implies a **deterioration** in the terms of trade.

(e)   Any two of eg factor endowment, access to advanced technology, demand conditions, structure and business strategy of firms etc.

Answer 11

(a)   (i)   ….. are levied on income or wealth.

        (ii)   ….. are levied on expenditure.

        (iii)   Income tax, social security contributions, corporation tax, business rates, council tax (any 1).

        (iv)   Value added tax, excise duties (any 1).

(b)   (i)   (a)   A   (b)   C

        (ii)   (a)   Income tax or corporation tax.

                (b)   Value added tax or excise duties.

Answer 12

(a)

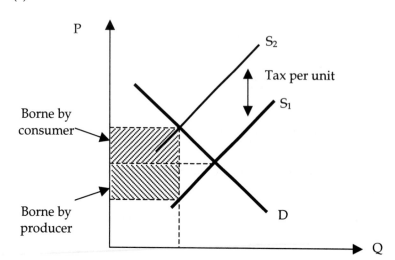

(b)   As tax rates rise –

     (i)   The price of leisure falls and taxpayers substitute leisure for paid work.

     (ii)   There is a growing incentive to look for ways to reduce the tax burden using tax avoidance schemes.

(c)   .... shift the business's demand curve out to the right, the extent depending on the income elasticity of demand. Productivity may increase.

Answer 13

(a)   (i)   A sustained rise in the general level of prices.

     (ii)   Those seeking but unable to find jobs.

     (iii)   The increase in a country's per capita national income.

     (iv)   Part of balance of payment recording exports and imports.

(b)   .... would become **larger**. There would be an **improvement** in all or most of the economic indicators.

(c)   Any three from: structural, technological, frictional, seasonal, cyclical/Keynesian, real wage/classical.

(d)   (i)   Claimant count – those unemployed and claiming benefits.

     (ii)   Labour force survey – those out of work and seeking employment based on survey data.

(e)

Raising the rate of income tax will reduce unemployment	*True or False*
Raising the rate of unemployment benefit will reduce unemployment	*True or False*
Raising the rate of interest will reduce unemployment	*True or False*

Answer 14

(a)   … total global **supply** has expanded more rapidly than global **demand**. This has led to an **increase** in coffee stocks and **downward** pressure on price levels.

(b)

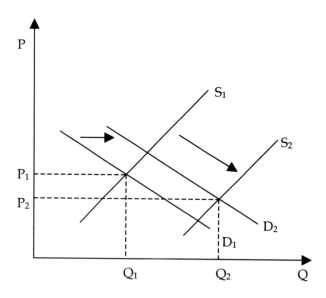

(c)   (i)   …. is a measure of the responsiveness of demand to changes in income.

        (ii)   High.

        (iii)   ….. grade coffee is **high** because …… it is a luxury good so as incomes rise more high grade coffee is bought.

(d)   (i)   When price falls below average variable cost.

        (ii)   It will rise.

        (iii)   It will be positive.

Answer 15

(a)   (i)   ….. is a cost imposed on third parties by the economic activities of others.

        (ii)   competition, pollution etc.

(b)   (i)   Price b, output h

        (ii)   Price c, output I

        (iii)   efg

(c)   (i)   An environmental tax to equal the cost of a negative externality (or … to raise private costs to the level of social costs).

        (ii)   fj

(d) (i)   ... the D curve shows the value consumers place on consuming an extra unit.

     (ii)   ..... the S curve is the MC curve above AVC.

     (iii) Marginal external costs.

Answer 16

(a) (i)   Claimant count and labour force survey (ILO).

     (ii)   Labour force survey.

     (iii) Not everyone looking for work claims unemployment benefit.

     (iv)   .. adjusted to remove regular seasonal changes so the underlying trend can be clearly seen.

     (v)   Cutting interest rates will boost aggregate demand so raising output and employment

(b)

Changing interest rates to affect unemployment
is mainly a demand side policy   (True) or False

Making credit more easily available will
reduce unemployment   (True) or False

Increasing income tax will reduce unemployment   True or (False)

(c)

Type	Cause
Structural	Decline of staple industry
Cyclical	Downturn in economic cycle
Demand-deficient	Insufficient demand
Technological	Introduction of new technology
Frictional	Time lag between jobs
Seasonal	Due to seasonal demand for labour
Real wage/classical	Real wages too high

Multiple Choice Answers

1.1   **B**

The fundamental economic problem is one of scarcity and choice: resources are scarce relative to human wants. Therefore the answer is B. Don't be tempted to choose D: always look for the best possible answer from the four alternatives.

1.2   **A**

Almost the same as question 1.1.

1.3   **D**

A, B and C are all true statements: it is D which is untrue. Choice is necessary because of *unlimited* (not limited) consumer wants.

1.4   **B**

The central economic problem is how to allocate scarce resources given that wants are infinite.

1.5   **A**

One of the three basic economic problems is what, and how much, to produce.

1.6   **D**

D is the standard definition of an opportunity cost: A is not such a precise answer and should not be chosen.

1.7   **C**

It is important to select the best possible answer, given that opportunity costs are about scarcity and choice, and the next best alternative foregone; so C is the answer.

1.8   **D**

Although A and B would increase output and C increase demand, only D will increase a country's productive potential.

1.9   **D**

A rise in the rate of investment and/or a rise in output per worker will lead to an increase in the maximum potential output which an economy is capable of, shifting the production possibility curve outwards. A reduction in unemployment merely moves the economy nearer its existing production possibility curve. A fall in the price of a factor of production is not directly relevant.

1.10   **B**

Welfare is synonymous with 'well being'.

1.11   **C**

Encouraging consumer expenditure increases aggregate demand, the others increase aggregate supply, ie economic growth.

1.12   **D**

A and B increase investment in training and therefore will lead to increased productivity. Similarly, C will ensure employees are treated fairly and are therefore more productive. D may encourage people to work, but will not make them more productive.

1.13   **C**

This is a standard definition you should know.

1.14   **C**

The four factors of production are land, labour, capital and enterprise. Do not confuse the economist's capital with cash.

1.15   **C**

Be careful not to choose D: you only get long run normal profit in industries with free entry and exit – such as perfect competition or monopolistic competition. There is no tendency for long run profit to be 'normal' in oligopoly or monopoly, where barriers to entry protect abnormal profit. Normal profit exists when returns are just high enough to compensate entrepreneurs for the risks involved in a specific industry, so C is the correct answer.

1.16   **C**

The only incorrect statement is (iv). Be careful not to think (iii) is incorrect. After all, entrepreneurship is a factor of production, with a cost to society. Entrepreneurs have to be rewarded with at least normal profit, or they will not supply their services. So normal profit can be seen as the 'cost of entrepreneurship'. So don't choose A: choose C.

1.17   **A**

The price mechanism operates in all markets in a market economy. B is a definition of a command economy.

1.18   **C**

Directives issued by a central planning agency are used to allocate resources in a planned economy.

1.19   **C**

Another question where it would be easy to make the wrong choice. Of course, the supply of factors of production will influence resource allocation, but it is determined mainly by the pattern of consumer expenditure: so the answer is C.

1.20   **B**

Profit is not a signal to consumers: consumers are concerned about product quality and price, not producers' profits.

Answer 2

2.1   **B**

A is derived demand, C and D are distractors.

2.2   **D**

This will cause a contraction in demand: A, B and C will all lead to an increase in demand.

2.3   **A**

This statement is clearly false and based on a confusion of cause and effect. Although an increase in demand causes an increase in the equilibrium price of a good, an increase in price will cause a contraction in demand.

2.4   **C**

A, B and D all cause a decrease in demand. Be careful about D: for normal goods, a decrease in income taxation would increase demand, but for an inferior good there will be a decrease in demand. C is the correct answer since a decrease in the price of the product causes an extension in demand (not a decrease in demand).

2.5   **B**

A rise in price would cause a movement along the curve, not a shift in the whole curve.

2.6   **C**

A shifts the supply curve to the right; B is a movement down the demand curve; D shifts the demand curve to the left. C is an increase in demand (at least if we assume a normal good), shifting the demand curve to the right.

2.7   **D**

A shifts the supply curve to the right; B is a movement down the demand curve; C shifts the demand curve to the left. D is an increase in demand (as consumers switch away from the close substitute good), shifting the demand curve to the right.

2.8   **D**

A and B will shift supply to the right and C is the effect of supply shifting to the right.

2.9   **A**

B and C would cause the supply curve to shift to the right. D would cause a shift in the demand curve.

2.10   **D**

This will cause a contraction in supply: A, B and C will all lead to an increase in supply.

2.11   **D**

An increase in the price of coffee leads to a rise in the demand for tea, since they are substitute products.

2.12   **C**

A and B would be caused by movement along the demand curve. D would be caused by a decrease in demand.

2.13   **A**

A is the correct definition.

2.14   **B**

As A and C are substitutes, and B and C are complements, a rise in the price of C will mean less C is demanded. Therefore more A and less B will be demanded.

2.15   **B**

A is producer surplus. C is community surplus and D is super profit.

2.16   **C**

The price mechanism (demand and supply) does determine the allocation of resources, factor rewards and the types of goods and services produced. It does not determine the preferences of consumers. In fact, it is the other way around. The preferences of consumers determine which goods and services there is a demand for. The answer is C.

2.17   **D**

A maximum price will only affect the market if it is below the equilibrium price.

2.18   **A**

Fixing a maximum rent below the equilibrium rent will lead to landlords taking their properties off the market. The excess demand will be diverted to other housing markets.

2.19   **C**

An indirect tax being introduced for the first time (or increased to a higher rate) is an unfavourable change in one of the conditions of supply, causing a decrease in the market supply of a good and shifting the supply curve to the left.

2.20   **C**

A are direct taxes. B and D are incorrect statements.

Answer 3

3.1   **C**

$$\text{Price elasticity of demand} = \frac{\text{Percentage change in quantity demand}}{\text{Percentage change in price}}$$

3.2   **C**

Where demand is price inelastic, quantity demanded changes by a smaller percentage than price. Therefore, total expenditure changes in the same direction as price. C is the only answer to satisfy this criterion.

3.3 **B**

Quantity demanded will change in a different direction to price, and by a greater percentage if demand is price elastic. This means that total expenditure will change in the same direction as quantity. B is the correct answer.

3.4 **D**

The proportion of income spent on a good (its budget share) is one of the determinants of the price elasticity of demand. When only a small proportion of income is spent on a good, changes in its price are unlikely to have a significant effect on demand, so that demand is price inelastic.

3.5 **A**

Another question about the implications of the price elasticity of demand for the effect of a change in product price on total revenues earned by producers (or total expenditure by consumers). Inelastic demand means quantity changes less than price, so that revenue goes in the same direction as price. Therefore, A is the correct answer. B and C both represent elastic demand. D implies unit elasticity (Ed = 1).

3.6 **A**

If the price elasticity of demand is less than one, then demand is inelastic. This means that *an increase in price* will increase total revenue (since the fall in quantity is by a smaller percentage than the increase in price). The drop in quantity will cause some reduction in variable costs, and therefore in total costs. So if revenue has increased and costs have fallen, profits must have increased.

3.7 **D**

If the price elasticity of demand is –1.5, then a 10% fall in price (from £1 to £0.90) will lead to a 15% extension in demand (from 10,000 units per month to 11,500). D is correct.

3.8 **A**

A fall in prices will lead to a rise in sales for all values of the price elasticity of demand except zero. It will lead to a rise in total expenditure on the good, when demand is elastic (Ed > 1). This gives us A.

3.9 **D**

If the price elasticity of demand is greater than one, then demand is elastic. A decrease in price will increase total revenue (since the rise in quantity is by a larger percentage than the fall in price). However, the increase in quantity will also cause an increase in variable costs, and therefore in total costs. So profits could rise or fall: *we cannot know, without information on the levels of marginal revenue and marginal cost.* So the answer is not B: it is D.

3.10 **A**

If the price elasticity of demand is greater than one, then changes in quantity more than offset changes in price, so that total revenue goes in the opposite direction to price. This means A is the correct answer.

3.11 **B**

Demand will be price elastic if a product has many close substitutes.

3.12   **C**

If the price elasticity of demand is less than 1, a fall in price will lead to a decrease in expenditure. This is because the extension in quantity demanded will not be large enough to compensate for the reduction in price per unit.

3.13   **B**

Draw two diagrams. On each one there should be the same two supply curves, representing an increase in supply (a shift in the supply curve to the right). Now draw on an elastic (quite flat) demand curve in the first diagram, and an inelastic (steep) demand curve in the second diagram. You will see that the equilibrium price has fallen as a result of the shift in the supply curve more in the second diagram (inelastic demand) than in the first (elastic demand). This is because an increase in supply causes an excess supply at the initial price, leading to a fall in price until there has been a big enough extension in demand to restore equilibrium again. Where demand is inelastic, this fall in price will have to be greater. So B is the answer.

3.14   **C**

The elasticity of supply is a measure of the responsiveness of supply to changes in price; it does tend to be higher for manufactured goods than for primary products (since it is difficult to change output of primary products significantly) in the short run); and it does vary with time (being greater in the long run then in the short run). It is not a measure of changes in supply due to greater efficiency (it has nothing directly to do with efficiency. So C is the answer.

3.15   **B**

The more inelastic demand is, the greater the effect of a shift in supply on price.

3.16   **A**

A positive cross elasticity of demand between two products means that an increase in the price of one leads to an increase in the demand for the other: they are substitutes.

3.17   **A**

A negative cross elasticity of demand between two products means that an increase in the price of one leads to a decrease in the demand for the other: they are complements.

3.18   **C**

An indirect tax involves a shift in the market supply curve to the left. If you draw two diagrams, one with an elastic (flat) demand curve, the other with an inelastic (steep) demand curve, you will see that market price rises more when demand is price inelastic. This is because sellers can shift more of the burden of an indirect tax onto buyers in the form of an increased price, when demand is less responsive to changes in price (ie less elastic, or more inelastic).

3.19   **B**

The more inelastic demand is, the more the burden of tax falls upon consumers. If demand is totally inelastic, the market price rises by the whole amount of the tax. The same is true the more elastic supply is.

3.20   **B**

An inferior good is one people buy less of as their incomes increase. In other words, a good with a *negative* income elasticity of demand.

Answer 4

4.1   **D**

Corporation tax is a tax on profits, not a cost. So the answer is D. B is not the answer: normal profits are the cost of entrepreneurship to the firm, from an economist's viewpoint.

4.2   **B**

A variable cost increases as output is increased: this is true of the cost of raw materials. A, C and D are fixed costs, since they are not affected by short run variations in output. The fact that interest rates change over time is not relevant to the question.

4.3   **C**

AVC + AFC	=	ATC
7 + ?	=	10
∴ AFC	=	3
1,200 ÷ 3	=	400

4.4   **B**

The law of diminishing returns determines the shape of the short run average cost curve. Diseconomies of scale cause the long run average cost curve to rise.

4.5   **D**

The AFC curve falls continuously – it does not rise. The MC curve falls then rises, not the other way round. Total costs rise continuously. Therefore D is the correct answer.

4.6   **D**

The law of diminishing returns is concerned with short run costs; B and C have nothing directly to do with cost curves. It is diseconomies of scale which are the cause of decreasing returns to scale and rising long run average costs. So D is correct.

4.7   **B**

Average variable costs increase when marginal costs exceed average variable costs. Be careful not to choose D: average total costs initially continue to fall when average variable costs have just started to rise, due to falling average fixed costs. Also, do not choose C: we have been told nothing about revenue or profit in the question. It is B that is the correct answer.

4.8   **C**

This is a standard textbook definition. If you got this one wrong, you should revise the theory of costs very carefully.

4.9   **B**

A is incorrect because MC could be rising. C and D are incorrect.

4.10   **B**

A standard definition.

4.11   **D**

Marginal cost is dependent solely on variable costs, therefore is affected by changes in factor prices.

4.12   **D**

Fixed cost is constant as output rises; marginal cost initially falls, then starts to rise; average variable cost initially falls, and only starts rising once marginal cost has increased above it. It is only total costs which *always* rise when a manufacturing business increases its output. Therefore, the correct answer is D.

4.13   **C**

If the total cost curve passes through the origin, at zero output there are no costs , ie no fixed costs.

4.14   **B**

The law of diminishing returns applies in the short run, when at least one factor of production is in fixed supply. Do not select D: it does not have to be capital that is the fixed factor.

4.15   **B**

Returns to scale are concerned with the growth of an organisation in the long run.

4.16   **C**

The law of diminishing return is the fundamental principle in the short run theory of costs.

4.17   **B**

This question is similar to question 4.16.

4.18   **B**

This is one of those questions with very tempting incorrect answers, so be careful. You don't need to be a monopolist to gain economies of scale as your business grows. There is a case for saying economies may not reduce unit costs if cancelled out by diseconomies of scale. You could argue that an inefficient set of managers could fail to take advantage of the economies of scale which should be available. However, clearly the best answer is that economies of scale 'are possible only if there is a sufficient demand for the product'. So B is the correct response.

4.19   **C**

It is only (iii) which is not an external economy of scale, because it depends on the size of the individual firms (and not the scale or geographical concentration of the industry). (iii) is an internal economy of scale. So the answer is C (i), (ii) and (iv).

4.20   **D**

Diseconomies of scale are a long run phenomenon, causing the long run average cost curve to rise.

Answer 5

5.1   **C**

Normal profit is the minimum profit required to keep a firm or factor of production in its present occupation or use. In economics, normal profit is included in costs.

5.2   **C**

Similar to 5.1.

5.3   **D**

If a firm cannot even earn enough revenue to cover its variable costs, it will leave the market immediately.

5.4   **B**

See 5.3.

5.5   **D**

Standard definition of productive efficiency.

5.6   **A**

B is allocative efficiency. A is the standard definition.

5.7   **C**

The profit maximising output is where MR = MC. MC is always positive, and for MR to be positive demand must be elastic. The AR curve is the demand curve and therefore indicates price. When profits are maximised, average costs are not necessarily minimised.

5.8   **C**

A firm is productively efficient when average costs are minimised.

5.9   **D**

'Breakeven' occurs when total revenue equals total costs, ie average revenue equals average cost.

5.10   **B**

When price is constant, the demand/average revenue curve is horizontal and therefore equals marginal revenue.

5.11   **A**

Standard definition. B is breakeven, C is productive efficiency, D is profit maximising.

5.12   **A**

A is the obvious answer here.

5.13   **D**

The marginal revenue curve is only the same as the average revenue curve when price is constant.

5.14   **D**

When marginal revenue is zero, total revenue is at its maximum. Note that output and revenue are not the same thing (C).

5.15   **B**

A firm must cover at least its variable costs in the short run.

5.16   **A**

Long run abnormal profits depend on the existence of barriers to entry into an industry.

5.17   **C**

See 5.14.

5.18   **B**

This is the condition for a loss making firm to be covering its avoidable (or variable) costs in the short run.

5.19   **A**

This is the golden rule of profit maximisation: you must memorise the MC = MR rule before you take the exam.

5.20   **A**

Marginal revenue equals marginal cost is the golden rule for maximising profit: so marginal revenue does not exceed marginal cost at the point of profit maximisation.

Answer 6

6.1   **B**

In the short run the perfectly competitive firm can make a loss and need not be operating at minimum average cost.

6.2   **B**

In the long run the perfectly competitive firm makes a normal profit so C and D are false statements. A is not possible in perfect competition.

6.3   **C**

In perfect competition the demand curve facing the firm is perfectly elastic.

6.4   **A**

The supply curve of a firm in perfect competition is its marginal cost curve above average variable cost. This is because firstly marginal revenue equals price in perfect competition; secondly, a firm will therefore produce up to the point where marginal cost equals price to maximise profits; and thirdly, if price falls below average variable cost, the firm will supply nothing as it cannot cover its variable (or avoidable) costs.

6.5   **D**

Marginal revenue = marginal cost is always true for profit maximisation. In perfect competition, marginal revenue equals price (since the firm is a price taker), so price = marginal cost will also be true. This gives us D.

6.6   **B**

The other three examples are all oligopolies (industries dominated by a small number of large scale businesses): only agriculture approximates to perfect competition.

6.7   **C**

All firms charge the same price in perfect competition, because they are selling a homogeneous (identical) product to well informed consumers.

6.8   **A**

B is a monopoly, and D is a characteristic of a monopoly.

6.9   **B**

B is the only necessary condition.

6.10   **A**

A profit maximising price discriminator sets higher prices where demand is less elastic (or more inelastic). Be careful not to put C: price discrimination by definition is not based on differences in costs.

6.11   **B**

For price discrimination, you need at least two separate markets, with different price elasticities of demand in each market. Price discrimination is not based on differences in marginal costs, but in demand conditions. So the answer is B.

6.12   **B**

Price discrimination involves one organisation charging different prices to different customers for the same product for reasons unrelated to costs. Only B conforms to this definition.

6.13   **C**

When profits are maximised, MR = MC. As MC is always positive, MR must also be positive, ie the AR curve must be elastic. AR is demand and therefore indicates the price charged.

6.14   **A**

Since 1973, UK law has accepted a 25%+ market share for any single business as evidence of monopoly power in a market. Firms have average revenue above marginal cost and produce at below the optimum output in all forms of imperfect competition, so these are not necessarily indicative of monopoly power. Therefore, A is the correct answer. *This is a difficult question for most students to get right.*

6.15   **B**

External economies of scale relate to the size of geographical concentration of an industry: they are not barriers to entry faced by individual firms. The other three are all entry barriers.

6.16   **A**

Notice the similarity with question 6.17. Perfect consumer knowledge will make it easier for new firms to enter an industry, and so is not a barrier to entry.

6.17   **C**

Economies of scale and limited consumer knowledge can act as barriers to entry, restricting competition in an industry. Low fixed costs imply low entry barriers, tending to increase competition.

6.18   **D**

Fixed costs can be a barrier to entry. Low fixed costs therefore mean barriers to entry may be small. B and C will tend to discourage competition.

6.19   **A**

A straightforward question. Profit maximising behaviour is one of the main areas of our syllabus.

6.20   **C**

Be careful not to choose D: price equals average variable cost is the minimum condition for a loss making firm to stay in a market in the short run.

Answer 7

7.1   **A**

In oligopoly a firm will consider the actions of rivals when setting its price and output.

7.2   **C**

Oligopoly consists of a small number of firms; there is a preference for non-price competition; and there are entry barriers. In most cases, there is considerable product differentiation. So C is the answer.

7.3   **D**

If you have revised oligopoly carefully, you should remember that oligopolists normally prefer to avoid 'severe price competition'.

7.4   **C**

This is almost exactly the same question as 7.3.

7.5   **D**

There is not usually a high degree of price competition in oligopoly: oligopolists prefer to avoid price wars.

7.6   **B**

The oligopolist's demand curve is 'kinked' at the 'sticky price'. This price prevails in the market.

7.7   **A**

(i), (ii) and (iii) are all features of oligopolistic industries. Since long run excess (or abnormal) profits are usually available in oligopoly, due to the existence of barriers to entry, (iv) is not true in oligopoly. Therefore the correct answer is A.

7.8   **C**

Monopolistic competition involves freedom of entry, advertising, a downward sloping demand curve for each producer, but not homogeneous products. Products are differentiated in monopolistic competition. So the answer is C.

7.9   **D**

If you have revised monopolistic competition at all, you will be aware of the importance of product differentiation and brand loyalty in that market structure. Be careful not to confuse monopolistic competition with monopoly.

7.10   **B**

Demand is not infinitely (perfectly) elastic in monopolistic competition: perfectly elastic demand curves are horizontal and are found in perfectly competitive markets for individual sellers.

7.11   **A**

The lack of barriers to entry mean that super profits earned in the short run attract new entrants to the industry, so that in the long run super profits are competed away. The other alternative solutions are irrelevant to the question.

7.12   **A**

B, C and D are all external economies of scale. A is an internal economy of scale, dependent on the size of the company and not on its location relative to other companies in the same industry.

7.13   **D**

A, B and C are all examples of external economies of scale, which can result from firms being located closely together. The existence of a cartel is irrelevant to location.

7.14 **D**

This is a tricky question, because cartels often aim to reduce production, sometimes claim to standardise product quality, and may even claim to reduce consumer uncertainty. However, the main purpose of a cartel is to 'ensure that all producers charge the same price'.

7.15 **D**

Vertical mergers occur between firms in the same industry at different stages in the production process: in other words, 'the combination of a firm with its suppliers or customers in the chain of production'.

7.16 **C**

A horizontal merger is with a potential competitor. A and B are both vertical mergers: D is a conglomerate merger.

7.17 **B**

Price is above marginal revenue in monopoly (and in imperfect competition). Do not put C: 'price' and 'average revenue' are two different names for the same thing (so price always equals average revenue).

7.18 **B**

Average and marginal revenue are falling as quantity increases. In other words, the demand (or average return) curve faced by the firm is downward sloping. This is not consistent with perfect competition, where AR and MR are constant, and the demand curve is horizontal. So the answer is B.

7.19 **D**

It is only in perfect competition where the long run equilibrium is at the level of output for technical efficiency (the lowest point on the ATC curve).

7.20 **C**

This question is a slightly harder one. Small firms will be more common when there are constant returns to scale (no cost advantages for larger firms) and where the market for the product is more dispersed. Advertising and brand loyalty, and research expenditure, can be entry barriers, making it harder for small firms to survive.

Answer 8

8.1 **A**

The demand curve for labour is the marginal revenue product curve. Marginal revenue product depends on the marginal physical productivity of labour and also on the price at which output can be sold. So the answer is A.

8.2 **C**

A fall in the price of labour would lead to a movement along the demand curve, not a shift of the demand curve.

8.3 **D**

The cost of hiring 11 workers is £24 × 11 = £264. The cost of hiring 12 workers is £25 × 12 = £300. Therefore, the marginal cost of the extra worker is £300 - £264 = £36.

8.4 **D**

The length of training affects the elasticity of supply of labour. The wage rate is determined by the interaction of demand and supply. Therefore, demand factors also have to be taken into consideration.

8.5 **A**

Transfer earnings are the minimum required to keep the factor in its present occupation or use. This can be assessed as the earnings in the next best alternative job. £550 represents economic rent.

8.6 **B**

This is a definition of an opportunity cost. Be careful not to put C, which is a definition of marginal cost.

8.7 **D**

A's transfer earnings are £180 and his economic rent is £70. B's transfer earnings are £150 and his economic rent is £100. Statement D is therefore correct.

8.8 **B**

The demand for labour is derived from the demand for the final good/service produced by the labour. Therefore, if demand for the good/service is elastic, the demand for labour will be elastic. Also, the easier it is to substitute capital for labour, and the cheaper capital is, the more elastic the demand for labour will be.

8.9 **C**

A and B imply a less elastic supply curve of labour: D is irrelevant. C is the right answer because an individual firm can attract extra labour away from other firms in the same industry as it increases the wage rates it offers. As wages rise across the industry, the supply of labour into the occupation from elsewhere in the economy may have a low elasticity: however, if just one firm increases its wages rates, the supply of labour to it from within the industry may have a high elasticity.

8.10 **A**

The supply of labour to an occupation will be more elastic (responsive to changes in the wage rate) when there is more ease of access into that occupation (more occupational mobility of labour). B involves less ease of access; C and D are irrelevant. A is the correct answer – if skill requirements are low, it will be easy for many workers to enter the occupation as the wage rate rises.

8.11   **D**

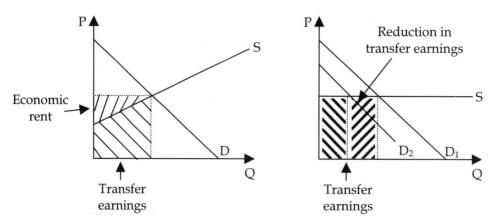

There is no economic rent if supply is perfectly elastic. If demand shifts to the left, transfer earnings will decrease.

8.12   **B**

Where the demand for labour is elastic, the imposition of a minimum wage will cause most unemployment. Do not select A: where the minimum wage is set below the market wage, it has no effect.

8.13   **C**

The elasticity of demand will affect the extent of unemployment. Minimum wages/ prices have to be above the equilibrium to have any effect.

8.14   **B**

Improved passenger train services will improve the geographical mobility of labour. (Option C, longer re-training periods, will reduce the occupational mobility of labour.)

8.15   **C**

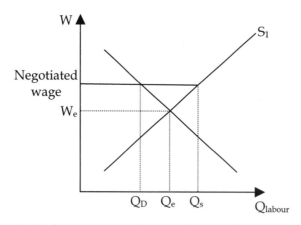

Q_D Q_e become unemployed. Demand for labour falls from Q_e to Q_D. The new supply curve is horizontal at the negotiated wage until it joins with the original supply curve.

8.16   **C**

C is the incorrect statement: increases in wages due to an increasing marginal productivity of labour, or to an increased demand for output do not necessarily lead to a rise in unemployment.

8.17   **A**

According to the marginal productivity theory, an increase in productivity will shift the demand curve for labour out to the right, so that the equilibrium usage will rise.

8.18   **C**

A rise in wages is most likely to lead to unemployment if the demand for labour is elastic, so that the demand for labour contracts significantly: or if the supply of labour is elastic, so that a lot more people will be looking for jobs. The demand for labour will be more elastic if the supply of substitute factors is elastic (making workers cheap to replace) or if labour costs are a high proportion of total costs. So (i), (ii) and (iv) are correct. It is only (iii) that is incorrect (if demand for the final product is inelastic, the demand for labour will also be inelastic, so that unemployment is less likely following a wage rise).

8.19   **A**

A trade union will not be able to win a significant wage rise without risking job losses, when the demand for labour is elastic. This will be true when labour is easily substitutable; when the demand for the product is price elastic; and when wages form a large proportion of total costs. So the answer is A.

8.20   **A**

This is a standard definition which must be learnt.

Answer 9

9.1   **C**

Unequal income distribution is an example of inequity, but does in itself cause markets to fail.

9.2   **D**

This is the textbook definition of externalities (external costs and benefits). Do not select A: merit goods generate positive externalities (external benefits). Do not choose C: these are external economies and diseconomies of scale.

9.3   **A**

The existence of significant external costs (otherwise known as negative externalities) implies that an item (often called a demerit good) will be produced in excessive quantities in a free market, since consumers will not be paying the full marginal social cost of the product. Do not choose B, which relates to external economies of scale.

9.4   **A**

Externalities are costs imposed by an economic agent or others. B, and C are obvious examples.

9.5   **B**

B is a standard definition and an example is public roads. A is a definition of a merit good.

9.6   **D**

This is the standard definition of public goods – items which are consumed collectively and from which no-one can be excluded as a penalty for non-payment (giving rise to the 'free rider problem').

9.7   **B**

Economies of scale are beneficial; and neither profit maximisation nor controlling a large share of the market is bad in itself. Governments may be concerned about monopoly power because monopolies 'restrict output' (to raise prices).

9.8   **B**

Be careful not to select D: there are specialist regulatory bodies like OFWAT for that purpose. The correct answer is B. Note that the Competition Commission is the new name for the Monopolies and Mergers Commission.

9.9   **B**

The only legitimate reason for preventing a merger would be a decrease in competition and rising prices (combined perhaps with a decline in product quality). Do not choose C: more concentration may increase competition, if smaller firms are merging to compete with a larger rival, or could reduce prices due to economies of scale. The correct answer is B.

9.10   **A**

Natural monopoly, public goods (where individuals cannot be excluded from consuming them), and merit goods (items with positive externalities) are all examples of potential market failure if their provision is left entirely to the free market. However, just because a good is a 'basic commodity consumed by everyone' is not a valid reason for producing the good in the public sector. Agriculture for example is clearly not suited to the public sector, even though food is a basic commodity. So A is the answer.

9.11   **B**

The price system clearly does not provide a distribution of income according to needs. This is one of the justifications for state intervention in mixed economies (a 'market failure').

9.12   **B**

Almost precisely the same question as 9.11.

9.13   **C**

This is a hard question. You might be tempted to select D, as external costs and monopoly power are examples of market failure. However, tariffs on imports are a further reason why resources may not be allocated in an efficient way. They artificially increase the prices of importable goods, diverting domestic resources into the production of those items, when those domestic resources would have been more efficiently utilised producing other goods. So the answer is C.

9.14   **D**

Similar to 9.10. A, B and C are all arguments in favour of state ownership.

9.15   **B**

The imposition of an indirect tax will shift the supply curve to the left and the market price will rise, but only if demand is completely inelastic will price rise by the full amount of the tax.

9.16   **A**

A price elasticity of demand of zero (perfectly inelastic demand) implies that the increased indirect tax will not reduce demand, since the demand curve is vertical (demand does not depend on price). This implies the maximum increase in tax revenue.

9.17   **A**

The allocation of resources is improved when the price of a demerit good is moved nearer to the marginal social cost of the good, using a tax equal to the external costs involved in the production of that good. B, C and D are incorrect.

9.18   **D**

Social costs of petrol consumption include congestion and pollution. A government remedy for this is to impose a tax to increase market price.

9.19   **D**

Privatisation is a means of widening share ownership; it does make industries more responsive to the profit motive; and it can provide a source of funds for the government. However, it does not permit additional economies of scale, and indeed the restructuring of an industry after privatisation to promote more competition can reduce the scope for economies of scale. So the answer is D.

9.20   **A**

Arguments for privatisation include encouraging an increase in productive efficiency; raising finance for the government, and increasing the flexibility with which organisations can be managed. They do not include taking social costs and benefits fully into account.

Answer 10

10.1   **B**

A, C and D are obviously not always true! As withdrawals are a function of the level of income, the statement in the question will be true.

10.2   **D**

Withdrawals include savings, taxation and imports: not distributed profits (dividends) or interest payments, which are flows of income. Therefore, D is the correct answer.

10.3   **A**

Equilibrium implies (investment + exports + government spending) = (savings + imports + taxation). Therefore, if investment is greater than savings (imports + taxation) must exceed (exports + government spending) to balance out the equation.

10.4   **D**

This question reviews the circular flow model of the previous chapter, and if you got it wrong, it is *essential* that you revise Keynes' circular flow model *now*.

10.5   **A**

Exports plus government spending plus investment (injections) equals savings plus imports plus taxation (withdrawals) is the condition for national income to be in equilibrium. Be careful not to select B: 'leakages' and 'withdrawals' are two names for the same thing.

10.6   **A**

Transfer payments are payments made not in return for any good or service provided. This includes educational scholarships, but not salaries of lecturers, payments for textbooks, or examination entry fees.

10.7   **C**

A, B and D are decreases in withdrawals, all leading to increases in aggregate monetary demand. C is a decrease in an injection, and so would cause a fall in the level of aggregate demand in an economy.

10.8   **C**

A, B and D are adjustments to give various definitions of national income. Only the value of intermediate goods are deducted to avoid double counting.

10.9   **B**

Statement B means that exports exceed imports. Therefore gross national product will exceed gross domestic product.

10.10   **C**

C is the textbook definition of gross national product at factor cost. A would be gross domestic product; B is irrelevant; D is net national product.

10.11   **C**

This is a standard definition. You need to know the elements of the main national income definitions.

10.12   **A**

This is a very difficult question. We might normally think of taking GDP at market prices, and then deducting taxes on expenditure and adding subsidies to get GDP at factor cost. Then we can add net interest, profit and dividends to get GNP at factor cost. Then deduct capital consumption to get national income (net national product at factor cost). If you go through this process in reverse, you will find that A is the correct answer. Be careful not to select C, which has factor cost and market prices the wrong way around. B and D are both nonsense.

10.13   **C**

The multiplier = $1/(1 - MPC) = 1/(MPS + MPM + MPT)$

A, B and D will all increase the multiplier: only C (**an increase in MPT**) will cause a decrease in the multiplier.

10.14   **B**

A, C and D are nonsense; only B is correct.

10.15   **C**

Net national product is gross national product less capital consumption (depreciation). A and B are nonsense: D is gross national product.

10.16   **B**

A, C and D are nonsense!

10.17   **A**

The multiplier = $1/(MPS + MPM + MPT) = 1/(0.25 + 0.10 + 0.15) = 1/0.50 = 2$

Or $(MPC + MPS + MPM + MPT) = 1$

So $MPC = 1 - (MPS + MPM + MPT) = 1 - (0.25 + 0.10 + 0.15) = 0.50$

The multiplier = $1/(1 - MPC) = 1/(1 - 0.50) = 1/0.50 = 2$

10.18   **A**

This is the definition of the marginal propensity to consume. B is the marginal propensity to import.

10.19   **A**

The multiplier = $1/(MPS + MPM + MPT) = 1/(0.2 + 0.1 + 0.1) = 1/0.4 = 2.5$

10.20   **D**

A marginal propensity to consume of 0.6 implies a multiplier of 2.5, so that a £2 billion increase in exports will cause a £5 billion rise in national income (exports being an injection into the circular flow).

Answer 11

11.1   **D**

A occurs in a slump, B in a recession and C in a period of recovery.

11.2   **D**

A, B and C all arise when the economy is recovering after a recession. Governments tend to borrow during a recession in an attempt to boost aggregate demand.

11.3   **A**

If interest rates fall, people have more money to spend and firms find more projects profitable, so demand increases.

11.4   **D**

A standard definition.

11.5   **A**

A is a definition of structural unemployment.   B and C both relate to cyclical unemployment and D is seasonal unemployment.

11.6   **A**

B will lead to demand-deficient unemployment, C and D to cyclical.

11.7   **A**

Technological unemployment can be seen as a form of structural unemployment, since technological change does not reduce the demand for labour overall, but changes the structure of the demand for labour in the economy.

11.8   **B**

C is the claimant count, A and D are not relevant.

11.9   **D**

A and C refer to seasonal unemployment, B to structural unemployment.

11.10   **D**

Unemployment caused by a lack of demand during a recession is cyclical unemployment (sometimes called Keynesian or demand deficiency unemployment). A is seasonal unemployment; B is technological (and structural); C is supply side.

11.11   **A**

The Quantity Theory of Money will not apply if the velocity of circulation is inversely dependent on the money supply, because a falling velocity of circulation of money could offset any rise in the money supply so that there was no rise in aggregate demand or the price level.

11.12   **C**

The value of money will fall in a period of inflation, so by the time the debt is repaid the money will be less in purchasing power terms.

11.13   **D**

This is a description of the accelerator theory: if you got this question wrong, you need to look at the accelerator and the trade cycle carefully.

11.14   **C**

A is the multiplier; D is the banking multiplier; B is not quite right.   C is correct; the accelerator is the amount of net investment (the increase in the amount of capital) necessary to increase productive capacity by one unit.

11.15   **A**

A is an advantage in the sense that a fair distribution of income in an economy is considered to be an economic goal.

11.16 D

D is the only example here of an increase in aggregate monetary demand. A reduction in direct taxation is a decrease in a withdrawal from the circular flow of income, and will increase consumers' disposable incomes. Therefore, it is the option most likely to lead to demand pull inflation.

11.17 D

This (D) is clearly the best definition here: the others are nonsense. Be careful not to put A or C due to misreading them, or B due to a confusion between the trade deficit and the government budget deficit.

11.18 A

C and D appear on the capital account: B is a credit item on the current account. Only A is a debit on the current account (an outflow of interest income).

11.19 D

They are all invisibles on the current account except 'inflows or capital investment', which is an increase in external liabilities on the capital account.

11.20 D

A, B and C will all appear on the current account.

Answer 12

12.1 C

A deflationary (tight) fiscal policy is designed to slow down the growth in aggregate demand, in order to lessen the pressure for demand pull inflation. Higher government expenditure will do the opposite: it is reflationary (loose) fiscal measure.

12.2 B

An expansionary fiscal policy aims to increase demand. If there is a low marginal propensity to save there will be a high marginal propensity to consume so the effect of, for example, lower rates of income tax will lead to most of the extra income received being spent. A would lead to increased imports, not affecting domestic output.

12.3 B

A contractionary fiscal policy will lead to reduced incomes so producers selling goods with a high income elasticity of demand will suffer. A would be the answer if there was a contractionary monetary policy with high interest sales.

12.4 A

A fall in exports or a rise in imports will reduce the circular flow of income and aggregate monetary demand, and therefore may decrease inflationary pressure. Tax cuts or higher public spending would do the opposite. So the answer is A.

12.5   D

Monetarists believe that inflation is caused by a prior increase in the money supply. When the government increases the money supply, people find themselves with larger money balances than they need and spend the excess, so providing the mechanism by which prices are pulled up.

12.6   C

Inflation raises domestic prices, so leading to a loss of international competitiveness. Inflation tends to increase government tax revenue and encourages borrowing (not lending).

12.7   A

A is a supply side policy, designed to decrease the natural rate of unemployment.

12.8   B

Supply side policies to reduce unemployment include anything to increase the quantity and/or quality of the labour force.

12.9   D

The term 'real' in economics always means 'adjusted for inflation'.

12.10   A

'Crowding out' refers to the displacement of private sector spending.

12.11   B

A rise in interest rates will make fewer projects worthwhile, so investment will fall. A rise in interest rates will make saving more attractive as opposed to shareholdings, so share prices will fall. A higher domestic interest rate will attract foreign savings, so the exchange rate will rise (increased demand for the domestic currency).

12.12   D

An increase in public sector borrowing will increase the demand for loanable funds, and put upwards pressure on interest rates. It may result from a reduction in taxation, but will not be the cause of a reduction in taxation. If anything, it will cause an increase in inflationary pressures, and expectations of higher inflation and rising interest rates are likely to push share prices down.

12.13   D

A and B are ways of reducing a budget deficit, rather than financing it. C may be a consequence of a large deficit developing. An issue of government savings certificates is one way of financing a deficit: so D is the answer.

12.14   B

Direct taxes are progressive: indirect taxes are regressive. An increase in progressive taxes, combined with a decrease in regressive taxes, is most likely to contribute to a decrease in inequality: so B is the answer. You may be tempted to select A, but B is clearly the better response (since A does not involve a fall in regressive taxation).

12.15 **D**

D is the definition of a regressive tax: it is not the amount of money, but the proportion of income paid which determines whether a tax is progressive or regressive.

12.16 **B**

A and C are nonsense; D is a proportional tax system. B is the definition of a progressive tax system.

12.17 **C**

A fall in interest rates may cause a rise in the demand for credit and in the demand for housing. It is also likely to help reduce government expenditure. The cost of interest payments on short term government debt will fall, and if low interest rates help to reduce unemployment, spending on benefits will also fall. Lower interest rates should help to increase investment, not cause a fall in investment: so C is the answer.

12.18 **A**

The transactions demand for money depends mainly on the level of consumers' incomes (which of course determine how much consumers plan to spend on transactions).

12.19 **B**

All will reduce demand pull inflation, except for the decrease in interest rates, which is a reflationary monetary policy likely to stimulate aggregate demand, and to add to demand pull pressures.

12.20 **D**

Both (i) and (ii) involve a deflationary fiscal policy; (iv) is a deflationary monetary policy. (iii) will not only decrease competition faced by domestic producers of importable products but will also decrease imports (a decrease in a withdrawal from the circular flow of income), tending to increase aggregate monetary demand and demand pull inflation.

Answer 13

13.1 **D**

A refers to money as a means of exchange, B as a store of value and C as a unit of account.

13.2 **A**

Portability is a quality of money, not a function.

13.3 **B**

The functions of money are as a medium of exchange, a store of value, a unit of account, and a standard of deferred payment (not as a measure of liquidity).

13.4 **C**

The broad money supply measure includes coins, notes and bank deposits.

13.5   **C**

13.6   **D**

The demand for money will rise if there is an increase in disposable incomes (increasing the transactions demand for money); a fall in interest rates (reducing the opportunity cost of holding money); or an expectation of falling share prices (increasing the speculative demand for money). A decrease in the money supply will not cause a rise in the demand for money.

13.7   **A**

B, C and D are all consistent with a deflationary monetary policy, designed to reduce the rate of growth of the money supply. A is not: central bank purchases of bills on the open market will put cash into circularisation, increasing the money supply.

13.8   **C**

Sales of government securities by the central bank (sometimes called 'overfunding' if these sales are not necessary to finance a government budget deficit) take money out of circulation (as investors use their bank deposits to pay for the securities), reducing the money supply. The other three options are all likely to increase the money supply.

13.9   **B**

Let the cash required be C.

$$\frac{C}{20\%} = 50 + c$$

$$C = 20\% \times (50 + C)$$

$$= 10 + 20\%C$$

$$0.8C = 10$$

$$C = \frac{10}{8} \times 10$$

$$= \text{£12.5m}$$

13.10   **A**

The Fisher Equation is $M \times V = P \times T$. When looking at percentage changes, you add the variables rather than multiplying. If m = percentage change in the money supply; v = percentage change in the velocity of circulation of money; p = rate of inflation; and t = rate of economic growth (growth of real output), then:

$$m + v = p + t$$

so $t = m + v - p = 25\% + (-5\%) - 11\% = 9\%$

13.11   **B**

Issuing gilts is a function of the Bank of England.

13.12   **B**

Commercial banks and building societies are deposit taking financial institutions and credit card companies specialise in lending.

13.13   **C**

Retail banks specialise in accepting deposits, money transmission and providing loans, not providing equity capital.

13.14   **A**

Advances to customers are the least liquid, the most risky and therefore the most profitable of these assets. Balances with the central bank (the Bank of England) pay no interest: money at call (short term money market deposits) and treasury bills (short term government debt) offer only low rates of interest.

13.15   **C**

For many years now, building societies have been able to offer full cheque accounts and money transmission services, just like commercial banks.

13.16   **C**

A, B and D are assets: customers' deposits are a liability to a bank.

13.17   **B**

Central banks can issue notes and coins, hold foreign exchange reserves and supervise the banking system (although the Bank of England no longer performs the last of these functions in the UK). Central banks do not conduct fiscal policy: it is government finance ministries – the Treasury in the UK – which make expenditure plans and revise tax systems.

13.18   **C**

Almost exactly the same as question 13.16.

13.19   **B**

Many people would get this question wrong, which is understandable because you need to read it very carefully. Investment trusts, insurance companies and pension funds all buy and sell shares in other companies. Stock exchanges do not: a stock exchange provides a framework within which shares can be bought and sold, but does not engage in buying and selling shares itself.

13.20   **A**

The benefits of financial intermediation are not dependent on a rising stock market, and do not directly imply a rising stock market.

Answer 14

14.1   **A**

Falling domestic interest rates may cause an outflow of hot money (speculative capital) from the country, an increase in the supply of the currency on the foreign exchange market, and consequently a fall in its price (exchange rate depreciation). B, C and D can all put upward pressure on a currency.

14.2   **A**

Floating exchange rates increase uncertainty and transactions costs and give governments more freedom to adopt expansionary policies, since there is no fixed exchange rate target for them to maintain. However, at least in the long run, they do provide automatic correction for balance of payments surpluses and deficits. If you have a large deficit, your currency will eventually depreciate, making your producers more competitive internationally and improving your current account position (subject to the Marshall-Lerner Condition).

14.3   **C**

The terms of trade is export prices divided by import prices – the best definition provided is C. It is not to do with volumes or total values, and is not the same thing as the exchange rate (although changes in exchange rates do of course affect the terms of trade).

14.4   **A**

This one is so easy you might get it wrong, thinking its too easy to be correct! *Yes, a cut in the level of public expenditure (government spending) is an expenditure reducing policy* (and a deflationary fiscal policy, in this case). The other measures are expenditure switching policies.

14.5   **C**

A and B should both encourage a rise in exports. D has no direct effect. C might cause a country's exports to decrease, as it implies other countries are spending a lower proportion of their incomes on their imports.

14.6   **B**

A rise in interest rates will tend to reduce share prices, cause a rise in the exchange rate and shift income from borrowers to savers: it will not cause a rise in investment (quite the opposite in fact, as the cost of financing investment has increased, and aggregate monetary demand is likely to start falling).

14.7   **B**

A devaluation will normally reduce a current account deficit (subject to the Marshall-Lerner elasticities condition); it should also increase domestic economic activity (assuming spare capacity exists), since it makes domestic producers more price competitive compared to foreign rivals. It will not improve the terms of trade, since it implies export prices are falling relative to import prices (often called a 'deterioration in the terms of trade'). It will not reduce the cost of living (rising import prices will increase the cost of living).

14.8   **C**

A fall in the exchange rate would not affect the domestic currency price of exports. It would mean that the price of exports measured in foreign currency would fall.

14.9   **A**

The WTO is about encouraging and policing multi-lateral reductions in trade barriers: not about encouraging customs unions and free trade areas consisting of only a few countries, or about providing funds to countries with balance of payments difficulties (which is a function of the International Monetary Fund – the IMF).

14.10   **A**

'Intra' in this context means 'within'. B is 'inter industry trade'.

14.11   **B**

Concentration of production close to markets runs counter to the principle of globalisation.

14.12   **B**

A similar concept to 14.11.

14.13   **C**

The benefits of trade are increased by economies of scale; large differences in opportunity costs, as a basis for specialisation; and low international transport costs. They do not depend on a high degree of mobility of capital and labour between countries, and indeed to an extent trade acts as an alternative to international factor mobility.

14.14   **B**

If you have looked at trade based on specialisation according to comparative costs (or comparative advantage), you will recall that it shows that trade arises because of differences between countries in the opportunity costs of production.

14.15   **C**

In the case of absolute advantage, a country should specialise and export the goods in which it has the lowest opportunity cost ratio.

14.16   **D**

As mobility increases, factor markets become more perfect and therefore factor prices will tend towards equality.

14.17   **C**

Economies of scale in production would increase the attractiveness of concentrating the production of a good in one location.

14.18   **C**

When a single currency is adopted, it is necessary for the countries concerned to adopt the same monetary policy.

14.19   **A**

If domestic interest rates rise relative to Euroland, investment in the UK will be attractive so the demand for sterling will increase, leading to a rise in the value of sterling. There will also be an increase in the supply of Euros on foreign exchange markets.

14.20   **B**

Common markets are customs unions which also allow the free movement of factors of production between the member countries. It is only in economic unions that common markets integrate further and adopt common economic policies.

Answer 15

15.1   **C**

A tricky opportunity cost question for you. The opportunity costs of the business include its £114,000 of expenses plus the £12,000 lease income forgone, plus the £15,000 interest income forgone, plus the £6,000 of extra salary Michael Dawson has forgone to work in the business (£14,000 less £8,000).

Opportunity costs = £114,000 + £12,000 + £15,000 + £6,000 = £147,000.

15.2   **D**

A production possibility curve (or production possibility frontier) will shift outwards when the maximum productive capacity of the economy has increased. Either the total quantity of factors of production available must have increased, or their productivity must have increased. A fall in unemployment is *not* going to cause the curve to shift outwards: it will merely move the economy towards its existing curve. Only technical progress – among the four options – involves an increase in productive capacity.

15.3   **A**

In a market economy, 'prices are determined mainly by market forces'. C is nonsense. D is clearly untrue, given the existence of oligopolistic and monopolistic industries. B would be true in a planned economy (not a market economy).

15.4   **C**

The factors of production are land, labour (including unskilled labour), capital (including a machine tool) and entrepreneurship. Cash reserves are *not* a factor of production.

15.5   **B**

A, C and D are terms outside your syllabus which need not concern you. This is clearly an example of opportunity costs – therefore B is correct.

15.6   **B**

Once again, to get this question right you have to remember that economics is concerned with 'the need to allocate scarce resources between competing uses'. The 'central economic problem' is just another way of referring to the 'basic economic problem' of scarcity and choice.

15.7   **C**

Economics is concerned with the allocation of scarce resources.

15.8   **B**

Similar to a number of other past examination questions, the key to this one is remembering that products are differentiated in monopolistic competition (and not homogeneous).

15.9   **D**

This question is not so easy. A reduction in an indirect tax (like VAT) will shift the supply curve to the right. As will an improvement in production which lowers costs. A fall in the price of the good will cause a movement down the demand curve (an extension in demand) and not a shift in it. The correct answer is D for the following reason. An increase in the supply of a complementary good will reduce the equilibrium price of that complement. A decrease in the price of a complement leads to an increase in demand for this product (just like a fall in mortgage rates leads to an increase in demand for property). Therefore, the demand curve for this product will shift towards the right.

15.10   **C**

A and B are irrelevant. D is a consequence of international trade and not an explanation for it. International trade based on specialisation according to comparative advantage is best explained by the fact that countries have different endowments of factors of production. Where cheap labour is abundant, a country will specialise in labour intensive products: where capital is abundant, a country will have a comparative advantage in capital-intensive products.

15.11   **D**

In mixed economies, resource allocation is mainly through the price system, producers do have an incentive to advertise and there is some government planning of the use of resources (which is why they are not free market economies). However, the term has nothing to do with there being a 'mix of small and large companies'. The answer is D.

15.12   **D**

Venture capitalists put money into high risk, new enterprises – partly in the form of equity. This is the type of rare question which is not worth specifically cramming for – you either know it or you don't. Students who read quality newspapers or magazines, like *The Economist*, are much more likely to get this type of question right.

15.13   **A**

Lower corporation tax or rising company profits will raise share prices, since they allow companies to pay higher dividends to shareholders. A decline in the number of new share issues will also raise share prices, by making shares more scarce. A rise in interest rates will tend to push share prices down, for a number of reasons:

♦   falling aggregate demand for companies' products.

♦   rising cost of servicing variable interest rate corporate debt.

♦   higher returns now being available to investors from interest bearing assets and deposits, rather than shares.

15.14   **A**

B, C and D are not true. The profit motive does encourage efficiency in the private sector, so A is correct.

15.15   **B**

The law of diminishing returns is the principle underlying rising short run average costs. Diseconomies of scale relate to long run costs, and the other two answers are completely irrelevant.

15.16   **A**

A high marginal propensity to save implies a low multiplier, so fiscal expansion will not have such a large effect on aggregate demand. Structural unemployment cannot be cured by expanding aggregate demand anyway. The exchange rate system is irrelevant to the question (actually, there are reasons to believe fiscal expansion may be more effective under fixed exchange rates, but they are way, way beyond your syllabus, and the examiner was certainly not thinking about them). The correct answer is A, since a high marginal propensity to consume implies a high multiplier, so fiscal expansion will have a larger effect on aggregate demand, and therefore on the demand for labour and cyclical unemployment.

15.17   **A**

A lack of incentives is not a market failure in free market systems: on the contrary, incentives are a major advantage of free markets.

15.18   **B**

A rise in price will increase total consumer expenditure, as long as demand is price inelastic (the price elasticity of demand for the good is less than 1). Quantity sold will fall, but not by enough to offset the impact of the higher price on total expenditure.

15.19   **D**

See question 15.9 and question 15.13 above.

15.20   **B**

This is the correct definition of an opportunity cost. A is marginal cost; the distinction between fixed and variable costs is irrelevant; in D, the opportunity costs of a business are above its accounting costs.

Exam Kit Review Form

CIMA PAPER 3a KIT – ECONOMICS FOR BUSINESS

We hope that you have found this Kit stimulating and useful and that you now feel confident and well-prepared for your examinations.

We would be grateful if you could take a few moments to complete the questionnaire below, so we can assess how well our material meets your needs.

	Excellent	*Adequate*	*Poor*
Depth and breadth of technical coverage			
Appropriateness of coverage to examination			
Presentation			
Level of accuracy			

Did you spot any errors or ambiguities? Please let us have the details below.

Page	**Error**

Thank you for your feedback.

Please return this form to:

The Financial Training Company Limited
4 The Griffin Centre
Staines Road
Feltham
Middlesex TW14 0HS

Student's name: ....

Address: ....

....

....

CIMA Publications Student Order Form

THE
FINANCIAL TRAINING
COMPANY
PUBLICATIONS DIVISION

o order your books, please indicate quantity required in the relevant order box, calculate the amount(s) in the column provided, and ld postage to determine the amount due. Please then clearly fill in your details plus method of payment in the boxes provided and turn your completed form with payment attached to:

THE FINANCIAL TRAINING COMPANY, 4 THE GRIFFIN CENTRE, STAINES ROAD, FELTHAM, MIDDLESEX TW14 0HS
OR FAX YOUR ORDER TO 020 8831 9991 OR TELEPHONE 020 8831 9990

or examinations in May 04 ❑ Nov 04 ❑ (please tick)

FOUNDATION

PER	TITLE	TEXT ORDER	PRICE £	EXAM KIT ORDER	PRICE £	FOCUS NOTES ORDER	PRICE £	AMOUNT £
	Financial Accounting Fundamentals		21.00		11.00		6.00	
	Management Accounting Fundamentals		21.00		11.00		6.00	
	Economics for Business		21.00		11.00		6.00	
	Business Law		21.00		11.00		6.00	
	Business Mathematics		21.00		11.00		6.00	

INTERMEDIATE

PER	TITLE	TEXT ORDER	PRICE £	EXAM KIT ORDER	PRICE £	FOCUS NOTES ORDER	PRICE £	AMOUNT £
	Finance		21.00		11.00		6.00	
	Business Taxation [FA 2003] (May & Nov 2004)		21.00		11.00		6.00	
	Financial Accounting (UK Standards)		21.00		11.00		6.00	
	Financial Reporting (UK Standards)		21.00		11.00		6.00	
	Management Accounting - Performance Management		21.00		11.00		6.00	
	Management Accounting - Decision Making		21.00		11.00		6.00	
	Systems & Project Management		21.00		11.00		6.00	
	Organisational Management		21.00		11.00		6.00	

FINAL

PER	TITLE	TEXT ORDER	PRICE £	EXAM KIT ORDER	PRICE £	FOCUS NOTES ORDER	PRICE £	AMOUNT £
	Management Accounting - Business Strategy		21.00		11.00		6.00	
	Management Accounting - Financial Strategy		21.00		11.00		6.00	
	Management Accounting - Information Strategy		21.00		11.00		6.00	
	Management Accounting - Case Study		21.00						

	Sub Total	£

stage and packing – please note a signature is required on
livery

K & NI   £5 for up to 10 books
          If only Focus Notes are ordered, £1 each (max £5)

	First book	Each additional book
urope	£25	£3
est of World	£40	£4

£

TOTAL PAYMENT	£

e following section **must be filled in clearly** so that your order can be despatched without delay.

TO PAY FOR YOUR ORDER TICK AN OPTION BELOW

I WISH TO PAY BY   MASTERCARD ❑   VISA ❑   DELTA ❑   SWITCH ❑

RD NO. | | | | | | | | | | | | | | | | | | | | (Some cards don't need all boxes)

PIRY DATE | | | | | ISSUE No. | | | (Switch only)   All cards - last 3 digits on signature strip | | | |

rdholder's Signature _____

rdholder's Name & Address: _____

Cardholder's Tel. No. (Day): _____

I WISH TO PAY BY CHEQUE ❑ Cheques should be made payable to *The Financial Training Company Ltd* and must be attached to
r order form. **Personal cheques cannot be accepted without a valid Banker's Card number written on the back of the cheque.**

UDENT NAME: _____

LIVERY ADDRESS: (Must be the same as cardholder's address. Please contact us if you wish to discuss an alternative delivery address).

ST CODE:		TEL. NO. (Day):	